# C⬤PTIVATE!

**How to use storytelling and brand archetyping**
to grab fans and increase sponsorship retention

Adam B. Nisenson

Published by Adam Nisenson and the Captivate Group
www.CaptivateFans.com

Cover Design by: Tuong Ngo

Edited by Beryt Nisenson and Veronika Lazabal

Printed in the United States of America

For my parents, who bought me my first Apple computer; and for my high school journalism/yearbook teacher, who introduced me to the magic of advertising and graphic design.

- ABN

# Contents

# Acknowledgments and the Blimp

I remember the day well. I must have been around 7 years old and it was the mid-70s. I was playing in my small, weather-beaten, wood sandbox in no man's land—a then undeveloped area that would one day be the heart of suburban Houston. Every house looked the same, as track homes had become part of everyday Americana. It was a Spielberg movie set waiting to happen.

When I first heard the loud humming noise, I didn't give it a second thought. Suddenly, the humming not only got louder, but the sun seemed to disappear. I looked away from the city of sand I was building, to see the most amazing sight floating over my head. It was the Goodyear Blimp.

A few years later, my Dad took me to my first major sporting event, a football game at the Astrodome. On the way into the stadium—through the noise of the fans that were having tailgate parties, through the sound of honking cars and the general chaos of the event—I heard that familiar humming sound again. As I glanced above the Dome in awe, I again saw the Goodyear Blimp. I was hooked. This was "Sports Marketing 101" before there was such a thing as sponsorship.

Now, what you need to know is that I had always wanted to be a professional athlete. But the good Lord only granted me with average speed and a 6-foot, 185-pound frame. Instead, I got a mind packed with a lot of creativity. So I took that ability, along with my passion for sports and did the next best thing: sports and sponsorship marketing.

I have been blessed through my career to not only work with some amazing people, but also to work with some of the greatest brands in sports (not to mention some great hook-ups for tickets).

So, this is where I want to thank my Dad for introducing me to sports, for connecting me to his passion for our home teams, and for using sports as a tool to connect with me and my brother. I am also so blessed by my amazing wife, who is not only an Emmy Award winning producer and writer, but one of my primary book editors (along with Veronika Lazabal).

I hope you enjoy my first book. My sincere desire is that through it you will learn new ways to break through the advertising clutter on behalf of your team, sponsorship or event. If you have questions or comments, please feel free to contact me at adam@captivatefans.com.

Wishing you a successful tip-off, kickoff, first pitch, faceoff or whatever you need to do to get started!

*"I always turn to the sports section first.
The sports page records people's accomplishments.
The front page has nothing but man's failures."*

Earl Warren

# The Passion
# of Sports

**Our teams and athletes allow us to experience the thrill of victory on a level that most of us would otherwise never get to taste.**

More than a pastime, sports have become the great American escape. It's not about free-throw shots, ringside seats or hotdogs and beer. It's about passion. It's about living and winning vicariously through a player, a team or a season. More than that, it's about human drama played out before us in a way that is, and always will be, more real than the most scandalous reality television shows. It's a personal, emotional investment that we make at the start of every game.

Consider this scenario:

There are eight people darting back and forth across a fifty-meter-long rectangular pool. There are no penalty shots, no extra innings and no halftime show. At the end of the race, there are no victory dances or dramatic climaxes. There are only competitors peering at the scoreboard to see who won, followed by an excited shake of a fist in the air. Doesn't sound like much of a spectator sport, does it?

Now consider this situation:

In the summer of 2008, the world sat riveted to their television sets as Michael Phelps broke record after record during the Beijing Olympic Games. With every gold medal, with every tearful podium ceremony, American pride swelled a little more. It wasn't just another win for the Baltimore Bullet; it was another win for our team. It didn't matter that, for the most part, we had never been interested in swimming as a sport, or that none of us really planned on following any other swimming competitions for the next four years. We had connected with Phelps— not only as a freestyle phenomenon, but as the hometown hero. We had invested a part of ourselves in every one of Phelps' swim meets throughout the Games.

That investment is a scene that is replayed every single day in stadiums and venues large and small across the United States. Fans faithfully follow their team through highs and lows, wins and losses feeling, if only for the duration of the game, a renewed sense of regional pride. They don't just watch a sporting event; they become part of the team.

And that is the heart of the American sports world. Every team, every player, every game has a story to tell. As fans, we're invited not to just read the story, but to participate. We've all been given a starring role, a front row seat and a chance to play the hero.

When the American men's team pulled off their 4-3 "Miracle on Ice" victory against the Soviet Union in 1980, it was more than just a hockey victory. Would "Sports Illustrated" have selected that game as the greatest sports moment of the 20th century if it had been just another intense match up? Probably not.

The fact is there was much more than goals, pucks and skates on the ice that afternoon. There was a story.

With the Cold War presenting a dramatic backdrop to the Olympic hockey finals, patriotic fever was an almost tangible element to the match. Fans waved flags and sang the national anthem. And then there was, of course, the most mythic of all plot lines—the underdog story. A group of amateur and collegiate U.S. players took on the best international hockey team in the world and won.

The fact is that we all have the will and the drive within us to win. It's archetypal. Our teams and athletes allow us to experience the thrill of victory on a level that most of us would otherwise never get to taste.

And therein lays the magic of sports branding.

Most successful marketing experts will agree that the toughest (and by far most important) part of any campaign is creating passion within your audience. You don't just want people to recognize your name; you want them to associate your brand with the same archetypal, zealous fervor that they feel for their hometown team.

The beauty of branding an event, team or sponsorship is that the fervor and the passion are already there. You already are the hometown team. Now you just need to tap into those emotions until the team, the game and your brand are so intertwined that the average consumer can't tell where one begins and another ends.

The ultimate goal of any marketer is to sell. But it's actually more important to create an undeniable (and hopefully unbreakable) attachment between the consumer and the brand. When it comes to branding your sports team or sponsorship, you want your story to resonate with the same intensity as the 4-3 U.S. win against the Russian hockey team.

All brands are not created equal. That's a fact that isn't lost on consumers. There are those companies that people turn to on rare occasions—when there's a sale, or when they believe that function or quality may be on the line. They might recognize the name and they might even turn to these brands on a semi-regular basis. But, in the end, the fans don't really care about them; they can take them or leave them. If the brand disappeared tomorrow, it wouldn't particularly affect them.

And then there are the brands that consumers follow with a near-religious loyalty. Regardless of price fluctuations or changes in formula, there is something almost reverent about the way people speak about certain companies. Have you ever heard someone talking about a product or brand name as if it were a close friend? (What red-blooded American doesn't consider McDonald's the ultimate in comfort food? And just try and separate anyone in Los Angeles from their beloved Starbuck's Mocha

**It takes innovative thinking to find the invisible connective tissue that binds sports fans to their favorite brands.**

Latte.) That's marketing gold, and the secret to striking it lies in making sure your customers are personally invested.

Following Michael Phelps' unprecedented Olympic wins, internet search engines reported staggering increases in searches pertaining to the Speedo Fastskin and LZR race suits.[1] With every gold medal won by Phelps, consumers became more fascinated with high-end racing swimwear. The public had, unwittingly, correlated the brand with his victories. Speedo had successfully pulled off the best move in the sports branding world: using the fans' zeal to sell products.

That move takes more than clever marketing techniques and glossy magazine spreads. It takes innovative thinking to find the invisible connective tissue that binds sports fans to their favorite brands. (And more importantly is the challenge to become one of those brands to which people feel bound.) Marketers need to give people the chance to become as much a part of the brand's story as they are a part of the sport. At the end of the day, every single company and sponsorship wants to be the Speedo of their market: the known favorite, the name people associate with the gold standard (or the gold medal, whichever the case may be).

But you can't get there if nobody knows who you are.

Enter the wonderful world of sports marketing.

It wasn't that long ago that the idea of branding a sports team or sponsorship was a foreign concept. Aside from a handful of thirty-second advertising spots on Monday Night Football, sports marketing was almost non-existent until the late 1980s. Today, team sponsorship and sports branding generate billions of dollars every year—and they show no signs of slowing down.

Why? Because it works.

Here is a look at a microcosm of the American sports world.

The 2008 men's NCAA basketball tournament had a total attendance of 763,607.[2] Spread out over 35 sessions, that makes an average per-game attendance of 21,817. That's nearly 22,000 chances not only to make a sale, but to possibly earn a fan's lifelong loyalty. Add to that the fact that all 21,817 people are already in the mindset to celebrate, have fun and, most importantly, spend money. Could your brand ask for a more perfect group to present itself to?

So, do I have your attention?

Good.

*"Half the lies they tell about me aren't true."*

Yogi Berra

# Storytelling in the Sports World: Myths, Legends and Lies

**Once people accept something as fact, it's next to impossible to get them to think any other way.**

The world of sports, much like the world of marketing, is more about perception than reality. It's not who you are; it's who people think you are. That's why storytelling, sports and branding go hand-in-hand. Stories are the original YouTube, a way to spread unbelievable tales to everyone and to assure them that no matter what anyone says, it's all true.

What is it about sports stories that draw us in? After all, even those who never bother to flip through the sports section on Sunday morning will stop and listen to someone retell a fascinating tale about last night's game.

Everyone loves a good story. Think back to your last cocktail party. Chances are there was one person in the crowd who stood out in your mind. He was the center of attention, the one who always had a good joke, an intriguing piece of trivia and a great story to share. That's exactly where you want your brand to be: standing in the middle of the room, surrounded by people whose attention you've completely captured.

### So, What's Your Story?

For as long as humans have had the ability to communicate, we've used stories to get our point across. Think back to when you were a child. No matter how many different methods your parents tried in order to teach you to stay away from strangers, the most effective one probably started with "Once upon a time … " ("Little Red Riding Hood" anyone?)

Stories, myths and legends live on long after facts and figures have been forgotten. Ideas conveyed in stories survive long after the death of the ideas that were carefully created in labs and boardrooms. No one ever lives vicariously through their favorite advertising executive, but we've all been motivated, captivated and fascinated by our sports heroes.

That's why sports stories are so popular; they combine the thrill of the win with the safety of the sidelines. That's also what makes storytelling a sports marketer's best friend.

In 1962, John Ford directed a movie that would come to be known as a classic American western film: "The Man Who Shot Liberty Valance." In the film, James Stewart admits to his biographer that he had been living a lie his entire life (he wasn't, in fact, the man who shot Liberty Valance). The reporter that's been interviewing him promptly tears up the notes that he just taken, much to Stewart's dismay.

The reporter's response to Stewart's malcontent is a marketing masterpiece:

"When the legend becomes fact, print the legend."[1]

It's a rule that is very much in play in today's sports and sponsorship world. Once people accept something as fact, it's next to impossible to get them to think any other way. It's that "stickiness" that will pull your target audience toward your brand and keep them there. All you have to do is come up with the perfect story.

Consider one of the greatest baseball legends of all time, Babe Ruth. Babe Ruth, in the fifth inning of game three of the 1932 World Series, was taking some good-natured ribbing from some of his opponents who played for the Cubs. As he came up to bat, he pointed to center field and then slammed Charlie Root's curveball nearly 450 feet to the deepest part of center field. It's the "called shot," and it's a sports story of legendary proportions.

Is it true?

No one knows.

More importantly, it doesn't matter. The legend became fact, and the rest is, as they say, history. If you can get people to accept your story (and, by extension, your brand) completely, then everything else is just details. Sports is perhaps the only aspect of American culture in which we are willing to accept the unbelievable as fact and where the astounding has become almost commonplace.

In the 80s and 90s, Michael Jordan rose to be known as the greatest basketball player of all time. Moreover, he became his own effectively marketed brand. Air Jordan started out as a nickname until the forces behind "His Airness" realized just how enamored the public had become with the story of the man who could start a dunk at the free throw line. All of a sudden, Jordan was much more than basketball. Shoes, sports equipment, Space Jam … everything Jordan touched turned to gold. The story fed the legend, the legend became fact and the story grew. That's an equation that leads to the perfect outcome every time.

Could Jordan really fly? Of course not! But it didn't matter. Fans were "stuck" on the story, and they couldn't get enough. Not that you should wait for R. Kelly to write a song about your brand, but you certainly can expect that your consumers will become your fan club.

**Consumers need to be emotionally invested in your story or it will be forgotten.**

### What Makes a Successful Story?

Let's start with what a successful story isn't: A good story will never be boring, predictable or full of fluff. In addition, it will never have been told in exactly the same way before.

That said, here are some tips on how to create a good story.

Keep your story simple or you will lose your audience before you even begin. Consumers have an ever-decreasing attention span. You have to make an impression (and fast) if you want them to remember your name.

For a story to be effective, it has to be memorable. People will never pay attention to a dull tale. It's just not going to happen. But if you generate interest, consumers will be tripping over themselves to retell your story. Create a need for information and then fill the need yourself. (Think parables, proverbs, fables and short stories with memorable characters and catchy punch lines. No one pays attention when someone tells them not to lie, but everyone remembers what happened to the boy who cried wolf.)

Think back to all of the really good stories you've ever heard. One thing that they probably all have in common is that they made you give a damn. Consumers need to be emotionally invested in your story or it will be forgotten. It has to be real. People are wired to feel an emotional tug, and it's that tug that stays with you.

On May 1, 1991, (exactly 100 days after his 44th birthday) Nolan Ryan of the Texas Rangers stepped onto the pitching mound at Arlington Stadium to face the Toronto Blue Jays, baseball's best hitting team at the time. Earlier in the game, Ryan had complained to his coach about feeling "every day of his 44 years." He felt tired. He had been told that he was too old to play. People didn't expect much from him that day.

Ryan went on to pitch the seventh no-hitter of his Hall of Fame career that afternoon.

There's the tug.

Finally, you need to find that connective tissue that binds your consumers to your name. Tell them a story. Razzle and dazzle them. Make them remember what you have to say.

In the summer of 1919, a racehorse named Man o' War was considered the greatest stallion to ever have run on the turf. Undefeated, he entered the race at Saratoga as the clear favorite.

Unbelievably, he lost.

The horse that won was an unknown. In fact, he'd given his trainers so much trouble in his youth that they had named the horse Upset. From that day on, any time that an underdog came out of the blue to win a match, it's been called an upset.

It's a tale that's been told over and over again. True? Who cares? It's a good story, and it stuck.

*"What counts in sports is not the victory, but the magnificence of the struggle."*

Joe Paterno

# Emotion and Sports Branding: Archetypes Explained

**We're all hardwired to subconsciously recognize and react to archetypes, whether we encounter them in literature, film or advertising.**

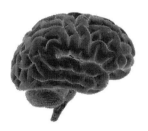

By definition, an archetype is "something that serves as a model or basis for making copies" (Princeton.edu).[1] In the early 20th century, Carl Jung suggested the existence of "universal forms that channel experiences and emotions, resulting in recognizable and typical patterns of behavior with certain probable outcomes."[2] In other words, characters and brands with strong archetypal features will unconsciously resonate with large audiences.[3]

Sounds about as exciting as root canal, doesn't it? But, believe it or not, archetypes are often a marketer's greatest secret weapon. They are, in and of themselves, the "magnificence of the struggle." We're all hardwired to subconsciously recognize and react to archetypes, whether we encounter them in literature, film or advertising. As our lives change, and as our personalities evolve, our attraction to certain archetypical patterns will increase. In other words, if you can identify the archetype that would resonate the most with your target audience, you've just dramatically increased the odds that consumers will feel emotionally attached to your brand. And when it comes to sports marketing, nothing fills seats like an emotional attachment.

Brands are the most powerful when they are based on an archetype, when they stay consistent to one archetype time after time, year after year. If you look at some of the world's most dominant brands—Nike, Apple, Starbucks, the Yankees, Harley Davidson and the Dallas Cowboys—you're likely to find an archetype at work. We'll dissect this powerful phenomenon here so that you can use it with your own team or brand.

Archetypes just got a little more exciting, didn't they?

Let's take a look at 12 common archetypes: innocent, explorer, sage, outlaw, magician, hero, regular guy/gal, lover, creator, jester, caregiver and ruler. Let's also learn how to recognize them at work.

## The Innocent

No matter what year you were born, you probably endured countless speeches from your parents about how much harder life was when they were your age. The fact is, in an ever-evolving, technologically guided world, most of us feel a sense of yearning for a simpler, more peaceful life. That's where the innocent archetype comes in. It's an archetype that represents everything we associate with the wide-eyed years of youth: simplicity, wholesomeness, naiveté, integrity and purity.

*Example of the innocent archetype:*

> At the 1996 Olympic Games in Atlanta, a baby-faced 18-year-old gymnast named Kerri Strug stood at the head of the runway before her second vault. With the weight of the team gold medal resting squarely upon her tiny shoulders, and with the Russian women's team waiting in the wings to swoop in and snatch the thrill of victory out of America's grasp, the stakes were clear: Strug had to land this final event, or go home empty handed. There was only one problem: Following a fall on her first vault, Strug had torn two ligaments in her ankle and could barely walk let alone sprint down the runway and fling her entire body weight up and over the horse. Casting aside her pain and all doubt, she appeared to be the very embodiment of youth and athleticism. As the world held its collective breath, Strug barreled her lithe frame down the runway with nothing more than a slight grimace to give away the severity of her discomfort, and executed a near perfect vault. Amazingly, she landed solidly on only one leg. A roar of cheers erupted before she collapsed to her hands and knees on the mat. The sight of her coach, Bela Karolyi, scooping up the petite, wide-eyed gymnast and carrying her to the podium to receive her gold medal is an image that is emblazoned on the memory of everyone who saw the event that afternoon.
>
> Strug, with both the trust and faith of a young girl and the courage and grace of a woman, was suddenly America's sweetheart. She

captured the hearts of millions of fans by embodying the image of the innocent hero. It was more than an event during the Olympic Games; for a while, at least, we were all feeling a renewed sense of optimism and national pride.

Other innocent brands:

- Ivory
- Disney
- Pillsbury
- Gymboree

## The Explorer

Huckleberry Finn. The Lone Ranger. Captain Kirk. Perhaps one of the most easily recognized archetypes—the explorer—abounds in literature, art and modern culture. From Hansel and Gretel to Indiana Jones, those heroes who search for a bigger and better world never fail to capture our attention. When it comes to marketing, the explorer is often the perfect way to tap into the desires of the modern business person, a person who is often trapped in a cubicle life. After all, who hasn't drifted off into a pleasant daydream after seeing a television commercial featuring a sleek sports car as it speeds along a winding road toward an unknown destiny?

*Example of the explorer archetype:*

> In 1963, a small group of sailors rented a basement in Chicago's tannery district and started to make and sell sailing equipment, duffel bags and rain gear. They had little to build upon; their capital consisted mostly of an adventurous spirit and a desire to show people the joy of the outdoor lifestyle. Within a few years, the entrepreneurial young sailors moved their budding enterprise to the rural town of Dodgeville in Wisconsin. There, among the rolling hills and cornfields, the company and the farming community went beyond coexisting as the sailors-turned-businessmen merged with the hands-on lifestyle of the countryside. The first outerwear catalog that they produced had a grammatical error in the name, but no one could afford to have it reprinted.

They kept the misplaced apostrophe—as well as the explorer mentality.

The world knows the company as Lands' End. Today, the company still thrives in the Wisconsin countryside.

The explorer is an archetype that appeals to us on several levels. Many people still hold on to the glorified ideas of exploration they had when they were young. (Could you ask for a better image than an association of your brand with a bed-sheet fort in the middle of the living room?) Also, as an archetype, the explorer taps into our desire to be something more, whether that "more" is a cowboy, an astronaut or a football hero.

Other explorer brands:

- Jeep
- Starbucks
- Levi's
- REI

## The Outlaw

There is a part of every one of us that, at some point, feels a measure of alienation, a need to rebel, a pent-up passion that just has to be expressed. Call it teenage angst, a mid-life crisis or "just going through a phase," but we are all outlaws at some point in our lives. The Godfather, Bonnie and Clyde, Scarface, James Dean—every outlaw shares certain characteristics. Chief among them is a sense of power that comes as they cause others to respond to them with fear and adoration. That measure of fear is important to the outlaw image because it taps into our own apprehensions about the shadowy underbelly of our society.

In the world of marketing, the outlaw has traditionally ridden his or her politically incorrect train straight into superstardom. For example, Harley Davidson has perfected its "bad boy" image and manages to make it appealing to cowboys, renegades, rebels and rogues of every age and social status. Even pent-up accountants and doctors have adopted Harley Davidson as their off-duty bike of choice. Likewise, Jack Daniels has built an entire empire on the idea that bad is better. And years after it hit the air, MTV is still giving parents grey hair.

When it comes to outlaws and sports marketing, no better example exists than a little NFL team known as the Oakland Raiders. With their rebel-like logo consisting of black and silver pirate colors, the Raiders are the most obvious example in the NFL, and possibly in the world of sports, of the use of the outlaw archetype. The Raider Nation (the unofficial name given to the team's faithful fan base) consists of some of the most notorious sports fanatics on the planet.

American journalist, author and devoted Raider fan Hunter S. Thompson once wrote that the Raider Nation was "beyond doubt, the sleaziest and rudest and most sinister mob of thugs and wackos ever assembled." Citation needed (Could a more perfect description of the outlaw archetype exist anywhere?) Anyone who has ever witnessed a gathering of Raider fans would be hard pressed to argue with him. Elaborately costumed, rowdy, and, on occasion, downright scary, the Raider Nation takes team loyalty to frightening new levels.

Something else that the Raider's outlaw image has caused to skyrocket? Merchandise sales. Three out of the last four years, Raider's gear has far outsold any other NFL team.

Other outlaw brands:

• Virgin Airways
• Johnny Cupcakes
• Juicy Couture
• Apple Computers


## The Magician

As children, we're taught that anything is possible. Later, as life makes us cynical, we lose that blind faith in both the impossible and the improbable. As an archetype, the magician's role is to remind us that the miraculous occurrence is not extinct and that no matter how hopeless something may seem it can happen.

Society has always been fascinated by the magical, the mysterious and the fantastic. From the nose twitching witches and scantily clad genies of 1970s sitcoms to the public's recent obsession with the "Harry Potter" novels and films, there's no denying that the metaphysical holds an appeal that's universal. The witch doctors, shamans and Merlins of years past have given way to ghost hunting reality TV shows, "Star Wars" prequels and sequels, and films like "Field of Dreams" in which Kevin Costner looks into the beyond for answers. Clearly, the magician archetype's allure remains as strong as ever.

Magician archetypes abound in the sports world, with figures like John Wooden creating Cinderella stories seemingly out of thin air. And then there are the most magical of all sports storylines—the last minute, come-from-behind victories. It's these magical moments in sports history that give us such a personal connection to our teams and players. American sports would be nothing without that connectivity between the great athletes and the common spectator.

*Example of the magician archetype:*

> On October 12, 2004, the MLB's playoff series began as the New York Yankees and the Boston Red Sox battled to see who would claim the title of American League Champion. Red Sox fans prayed for an end to one of the longest post-season droughts in the history of baseball. At first the seven-game series did not seem to bode well for Boston, as they lost the first three games and prepared to go home empty handed.

> Then, at the end of game four, the magical happened. Pushing the game into 12 innings, the Red Sox won 6-4. Fans barely dared to dream. And then it happened again in game five. When the Red Sox won 4-2 in game six, it almost seemed like a fairy tale. And when Boston blew New York out of the water with a 10-3 win at the end of game seven, at exactly one minute after midnight, Red Sox loyalists learned to believe in miracles again.

> The enchantment continued as Boston went on to sweep the St. Louis Cardinals in the 2004 World Series. They were the first team in Major League Baseball history to win a seven-game series after losing the first three games. The magic of that moment put baseball back on the front pages of the sports magazines and television shows that only months before had been ridiculing the sport's loss of popularity.

Other magician brands:

- Sony
- Calgon
- MasterCard
- General Foods International Coffees

## The Regular Guy/Gal

Does a larger target audience exist than the everyday Joe? Certainly, the huge success of country music should serve as some kind of indicator that the regular guy is an archetype to which people feel a strong connection. And television producers seem to realize that people need to connect with someone who reminds them of themselves. Some of the most successful shows in TV history are a beautiful celebration of the commonplace person (think "Roseanne," "Seinfeld," "Cheers," "All in the Family" or "Good Times").

Beyond music and the big screen, many other brands have learned to cash-in on the power of the regular guy/gal archetype. Saturn has built an automotive empire from the idea that, although they are car makers, they are still just everyday people. And any woman who has seen the most recent commercials for Suave shampoo (the ones that show a woman with salon perfect hair buying groceries, changing diapers and making dinner) probably felt a connection to the domestic goddess in the spots.

Many people cite the reason for ESPN's unparalleled success as a sports station to the fact that their anchors and sports reporters are, for the most part, regular fans talking about what happened during today's game.

Likewise, when it comes to our sports heroes, teams and brands, fans often feel a kinship for those players who most resemble them. It all makes us believe that we too could become a sports superstar.

*Example of the regular guy/gal archetype:*

> John Starks was working as a grocery bagger in Tulsa, Oklahoma before he decided to play basketball for several community colleges as he

studied. After being passed over in the draft, Starks quietly worked his way into the World Basketball League, the Continental Basketball Association, and, eventually, the NBA. In 1990, during a tryout for the New York Knicks, Starks tried to dunk on center Patrick Ewing (unsuccessfully) and fell, breaking his arm. Because of the injury, the Knicks were not allowed to release him, and ended up keeping the former stock boy on the team.

In 1993, John Starks became the key player in one of the most amazing moments in New York basketball history. During the playoff series against the Chicago Bulls, he pulled off a brilliant play, eventually driving fiercely along the baseline to dunk over the head of the much taller Horace Grant.

Not bad for a guy who a few short years earlier was just like millions of other hard working Americans. Paper or plastic?

Other regular guy/gal brands:

• Dockers
• Wendy's
• Snapple
• Motel 6

## The Jester

Has there ever been a time in history when we craved laughter more than today? We sit through informational programs, barely able to keep up with all of the impending doom that awaits us as we watch the ticker at the bottom of the screen deliver even more bad news. And yet the part of the program we remember most is usually the goofy commercial. Laughter is more than just the best medicine; it's also the best escape from reality. Smart marketers realize this fact, and the smartest of all are able to act on it. Take Geico, for instance. If a subject duller than auto insurance exists, you'd be hard pressed to find it. But two brilliant ad campaigns in recent years have done the seemingly impossible: They made talking about car insurance fun. Who doesn't love the precocious gecko with an English accent? And the "so easy a caveman can do it" commercials actually spurred their own short-lived television sitcom!

Of course, in the sometimes intense world of sports and sponsorship marketing, it's often difficult to find the levity required to tap into the jester archetype. But when it works, it's a very good thing indeed.

*Example of the jester archetype:*

> In the mid-1920s, a group mostly made up of African American men formed a basketball team on the south side of Chicago. Naming themselves after the center of Black American culture of the time, the Harlem Globetrotters began touring Illinois, competing in competitions throughout the state. Gradually, they began working comic routines into their exhibition acts until they became known more for their antics (and skillful execution of complicated moves and almost impossible shots) than for actually playing basketball.
>
> After nearly 40 years, the Globetrotters played their first "home" game in 1968. By then, they were superstars of the basketball world, bringing joy to fans across the country (eventually, they would go global as well).
>
> Many big name NBA stars who played for the Globetrotters have cited the time they spent spinning, juggling and tossing balls in front of thousands of adoring fans as some of the most satisfying moments of their careers.
>
> Not surprisingly, most people can't help but smile as soon as they hear the whistled tune, "Sweet Georgia Brown."
>
> Today, the Globetrotters play more than 300 exhibition games a year, always to packed houses. It's not just funny business.

Other jester brands:

- Got Milk?
- Miller Lite
- Ben & Jerry's
- M&Ms

## The Caregiver

Of the 12 major archetypes used in marketing strategies, the caregiver is probably one of the most audience-specific. While people of every background, social status and gender will feel an emotional connection to the nurturing, selfless character of the caregiver, women (especially mothers) are hardwired to react most deeply to this archetype's protective nature.

This isn't to say that only women can fall under the caregiver archetype. In fact, some of the most effective caregivers are created by juxtaposing an image of big, bad sports star and their nurturing endeavors. (Check out Chapter 13, titled "Cause Marketing," for more on this.)

*Example of the caregiver archetype:*

> Warrick De'Mon Dunn always felt a sense of awe for his mother. She raised six children on her own while working as both a police officer and, in her off-duty time, as a security guard. While there was not a lot of material wealth in the Dunn home, there was always a surplus of laughter and support, especially as Warrick's future in football began to take shape. The soft-spoken teen developed a passion for football, leading his Baton Rouge high school team to the state 4A championship for the first time in its history. Then, in 1993, tragedy struck the family when Warrick's mother was murdered while making a bank deposit after work one night. Two days after his 18th birthday, Dunn became the guardian for his five siblings.

> Even as his college and professional career took off, Dunn never forgot the way his mother had struggled to make ends meet throughout his childhood—and the way she had dreamed of someday buying a home for her family.

> In 1997, just after being drafted by the Tampa Bay Buccaneers, he established the Warrick Dunn Foundation and the Homes for the Holidays program. Geared towards helping single and struggling parents to achieve their own American Dream, these programs provide down payments for homes to families that otherwise couldn't afford one. Then (with the assistance of area sponsors) the program furnishes the homes, as well.

> In the aftermath of Hurricane Katrina, Dunn challenged all NFL players to donate at least $5,000 to the recovery effort. He helped raise over five million dollars for the cause.

> Today, the name Warrick Dunn is as synonymous with community service as it is with excellence in football.

Other caregiver brands:

- Johnson & Johnson
- Snuggle
- Band-Aid


## The Lover

Sex sells. The sensual, the erotic and the romantic capture our attention in a way that few other emotions can. Whether it's because of a biological need to mate or an intellectual craving to find our "soul mate," humans are undeniably drawn to the lover archetype.

Which is why nearly every product, company and organization has turned to sexually charged marketing techniques at some point (and many others have based entire advertising campaigns around the idea that sexy is better). From cars to liquor and power tools, a product doesn't have to be sexy in and of itself for the lover archetype to work.

*Example of the lover archetype:*

> In 1964, "Sports Illustrated" editor Andre Laguerre, frustrated with the way that magazine sales dipped in the slow winter months, sent out fashion reporter Jule Campbell to find something interesting to grace the magazine's cover and fill a few pages. Campbell's shoot, which featured model Babette March frolicking in the surf, caused nothing less than a sensation with the magazine's readers. A blatant exhibition of femininity and sexuality, many argued that supermodels didn't belong on the cover of a sports publication.

> Sales soared. The feat was repeated every year—and in 1997 the first full blown "Sports Illustrated" Swimsuit Edition was born. Today, it is by far the magazine's best-selling edition, bringing in close to $35 million dollars annually.

Other lover brands:

- Victoria's Secret
- Calvin Klein
- Godiva Chocolates
- Axe Body Wash

## The Sage

Galileo. Oprah. Albert Einstein. Walter Cronkite. Confucius. People will always flock to those who have the answers we're looking for. From scholars and teachers to researchers and detectives, the sage archetype is the one that unravels the mysteries, explaining to us not only what is, but why.

*Example of the sage archetype:*

> In 1966, the Oakland Raiders signed on an unknown assistant coach named Bill Walsh. Over the course of the next decade, he would serve as assistant coach for several teams (including the Cincinnati Bengals and the San Diego Chargers) and study the vertical passing offense favored by all of the big-time coaches of the time.
>
> Deciding that he could come up with a better way to play, Walsh developed his own offensive philosophy, one that favored a predominantly horizontal passing approach. These short, precisely timed passes came to be known as the West Coast Offense. That proved to be just the tip of the iceberg. In time Walsh became known as the "sage" of the football world.
>
> In 1979, Walsh was hired as head coach of the long-suffering San Francisco 49ers. Carefully studying the leadership styles of Civil War and World War I generals to fine-tune his own leadership skills, Walsh took his team from a dismal 2-14 record in 1979 to a Super Bowl championship in 1981.

Other sage brands:

- Harvard
- Deepak Chopra
- CNN
- Wikipedia


## The Hero

The most well-known of all common archetypes, the hero can be seen throughout all of modern literature and film. Whether it's the action superstar who regains his identity just in time to thwart a hostile world takeover, or the smooth talking attorney who manages to win her case and her lover's heart, you'll recognize a story's hero as soon as you come across it.

Heroes pride themselves not only on their discipline and focus, but on their uncanny ability to make the right decision in tough circumstances.

*Example of the hero archetype:*

> In 1991, a young American cyclist named Lance Armstrong won the U.S. Amateur Bicycling championship. The following year, the seemingly unstoppable athlete competed in both the Summer Olympic Games (where he finished in an impressive 14th place) and the Tour of Ireland race.
>
> In 1993, following 10 one-day events (and 10 wins) he became one of the youngest riders to win the UCI Road World Championship. In addition, 1993 also marked the athlete's first stage appearance at the Tour de France.
>
> But it wouldn't be his last.
>
> Between 1999 and 2005, Armstrong would win the Tour de France every year, an unprecedented feat. And when you take a look at where he was just three years earlier, the Lance Armstrong story is truly heroic.
>
> In October of 1996, at the age of 25, Armstrong was diagnosed with stage-three testicular cancer. The prognosis looked grim and immediate surgery and chemotherapy were required. He was given a less than 40 percent chance of survival.
>
> Not only did he survive, he went on to win the Tour seven times. He also created the Lance Armstrong Foundation, a non-profit organization geared towards empowering those living with cancer.
>
> To date, his Live Strong wristbands are considered one of the most successful cause marketing campaigns ever created.

Other hero brands:

• NASA
• Nike
• Federal Express

## The Creator

Like the outlaw archetype, the creator archetype is based on non-conformist ideas. But whereas an outlaw is driven by a desire to rebel, the creator's desire is to craft, build and express something new. Creators are artists, writers and architects who build immortality through their creations.

*Example of the creator archetype:*

> As the nation's largest publicly held insurance company, Allstate is widely recognized by consumers for their "you're in good hands" slogan. In the sports world, however, the Fortune 100 company is known for something else as well: their sponsorship of college football.
>
> At 67 different college stadiums across the nation, the "Good Hands Nets" are set up behind the field goals. Every time a field goal and extra point is kicked into those nets, the insurance giant contributes money to their collegiate academic scholarship funds. All in all, close to $2 million has been raised for incoming college freshmen since the program's inception.
>
> Another Allstate college football creation can be found in 2009's Allstate/FCA Good Works Team. Twenty-two college football players, chosen because they represent the spirit of teamwork, generosity and sportsmanship, comprise the two 11-member teams—players who are recognized for the good they're doing off the field.
>
> Through volunteer committees, foundation grants and responsible corporate citizenship, Allstate is creating an image for itself far different from that of any other insurance company today.

Other creator brands:

• Gateway
• Nintendo
• Crayola
• Home Depot

## The Ruler

When you think of the ruler archetype, think of someone who takes the lead. People like CEOs, kings and queens, and even moms and dads fit the ruler archetype because they rule their "kingdoms."

Likewise, ruler brands are organized, methodical and can even seem domineering. But it's the ruler's motive that makes such a controlling manner acceptable to others: The ruler is motivated to make the world a better place by maintaining control.

These ruler brands are often revered—and because of that, there are many "wannabes." Both IBM and Microsoft are good examples. But think about how many other brands have tried to emulate these industry trendsetting giants?

*Example of the ruler archetype:*

> The goal of a ruler is to create a successful and prosperous company or organization, as well as to reward loyal "subjects" with exclusive deals, offers and benefits.
>
> Perhaps American Express is one of the best examples of a ruler archetype. The credit card giant is famous for its member's only sponsored events and its platinum and gold cards, which were the first to distinguish a person's wealth by a card's color. Mercedes-Benz Fashion Week, the Tribeca Film Festival, and several Cirque du Soleil programs are among some of the events sponsored by American Express, along with such high profile sports teams as the Los Angeles Galaxy soccer team and the Los Angeles Kings.
>
> As the first credit card company to bring its cardholders the opportunity to attend events and receive prime ticket locations, American Express placed itself in a whole different class from every other credit card on the market, even though the competitors have followed suit. That makes them the ruling class of plastic.

Other ruler brands:

• Ritz-Carlton
• Cadillac
• The White House
• Rolex

## In Summary

Around 1919, Carl Jung suggested that everyone's psychological framework has innate and universal archetypes that affect the way we interpret and observe the world around us.

The use of these archetypal patterns can resonate with a marketer's target audience on a basic and subconscious level. When it comes to presenting your sponsorship or brand to the public, there is no better way to create an emotional connection with your public than with the clever use of archetypes.

*"If you don't invest very much,
then defeat doesn't hurt very much
and winning isn't very exciting."*

Dick Vermeil

# What's Your Brand?

# Does your target audience understand your message? Does the mass media communicate a similar story to the one that you're telling?

According to "The Business of Sports Management," a sports brand is defined as "The complete set of images about a sports organization held in the mind of the supporter."[1]

Those supporters are the very people whose attention you're trying to captivate. As you attempt to bind sports fans to your name, your brand will serve as both the lure that gets them to notice you in the first place and the sticking point that makes them stay by your side. But like all marketing techniques, a brand runs the risk of becoming stale and outdated.[2]

If you're not getting the kinds of results you'd like to see, or if your brand has never caught on with fans, then it may be time for a brand audit or a re-branding.

Brand auditing is the process of taking your brand and your marketing ideas apart and then checking them for consistency, visual appeal and cohesiveness. In short, a brand audit is a "check up" of your brand and its story. For more on brand auditing, see Chapter 5.

If you're thinking about redoing your organization's brand, ask yourself some key questions.

**What's my message?** Can consumers or fans pick up on what you're trying to say right away? Are you being consistent with your message, or is there room for questioning and doubt?

**Is my information current?** Outdated information and unchecked facts are big turn-offs for consumers. Is the information you are bringing to your target audience fresh and informative? Are you telling them what they need to know in a concise, informative and (most importantly) engaging way?

**Am I being consistent?** Are you following industry standards? Are you keeping a common look, feel, and vibe throughout all media and collateral material? Can your desired market relate to what you're trying to tell them? Is it basically the same each time they see it?

**Am I communicating well?** Does your target audience understand your message? How do you compare to your competition in their eyes? Does the mass media communicate a similar story to the one that you're telling?

If any of these areas need work or leave you questioning, then it may be time to revamp your brand. Think of your brand as a living, breathing entity. Without work and care, it will wither away, forgotten like so many others. But, with a little tweaking and a bit of a "makeover," it can emerge brand new and ready to resonate with your audience.

There are five major aspects of a well-developed, well-executed brand.

## Characters

Your brand is a story, and like all good stories it is made up of characters. How do these characters play out in your brand's story?

Your character profiles aren't limited to your organization's players, either. Remember, in the world of American sports and sponsorships, everyone is a persona—from the bleacher bums and season ticket holders to the executives and suits in the VIP boxes. If you want your story to resonate with your customers, then you have to really know who those customers are.

Understanding your characters is the key to creating a great story. So when it comes to your brand audit, start by identifying your potential customers. What brands are they already loyal to? How old are they? What do they do for a living? What do they do for fun? Doing your research will help you define your client base. This will help you design the perfect way to address their needs.

It's important not to try to be everything to everyone. Determining your target audience is probably the most crucial step to developing your characters and their story.

## The Walkaways

Simply put, the Walkaways are the statements—verbalized or not—that a consumer carries with them after an interaction with your organization or company. What did they think of you? What kind of impression did you make? Will they be back? Without a doubt, the answers to the first two questions will affect the third. Put yourself in the mindset that you would like a potential consumer to have. Now, what would they feel and think about your name? What would they associate with your name? How do those "ideal" Walkaway statements compare to what is actually happening with your brand?

Looking at your company or sponsorship in this new light might be the key to breathing new life into it. Let the Walkaways drive your marketing focus and your audience will inevitably pick up on it.

Walkaway examples:

- What an amazing experience my entire family had.
- The customer service reminded me of _____.
- The _____ really delivered on its promise.

## Archetype

If your brand were a person, who would it be? What would it say? Who would its friends be? The best way to begin profiling your brand's personality is with archetypes. Choose the one that best represents your brand and go from there. Are you going for a fun-loving, feel-good, jester-type personality? Maybe you want to convey the youthful exuberance of the innocent archetype. Or perhaps you are trying to harness the mystical appeal of the magician. Once you know who your brand is, it's easier to design what it should be doing. (Look back at Chapter 3 for more explanation of archetypes.)

## Personality

Once you've chosen your archetype, you should humanize your brand by describing it with the same words that you would use to characterize a person. Is your brand powerful, charismatic, fresh, youthful or daring?

Or would you say that your brand is more traditional, having strong, worldly and wise traits? Here are some ideas for personalizing your brand. (Feel free to choose your own, depending on what you need your brand to say.)

| ARCHETYPE | PERSONALITY TRAITS |
|---|---|
| The innocent | youthful, sweet, innocent, darling, fresh, angelic, simple, peaceful, childlike, hopeful |
| The explorer | free, individual, unique, fun-loving, adventurous, enthusiastic |
| The sage | worldly, wise, traditional, intelligent, analytical, understanding, truthful |
| The hero | courageous, brilliant, strong, charismatic, daring, worthy, powerful |
| The outlaw | outrageous, rebellious, revolutionary, shocking, wild |
| The magician | magical, universal, visionary, flowing, knowledgeable |
| The regular guy/gal | connecting, solid, real, authentic, virtuous, social |
| The lover | romantic, sweet, pleasurable, seductive, passionate, appreciative |
| The jester | fun, clever, youthful, joyous, enjoyable, indulgent, funny, silly, light |
| The caregiver | compassionate, generous, caring, warm, tender |
| The creator | artistic, emotional, creative, dramatic, imaginative |
| The ruler | successful, responsible, social, leader, prosperous, authoritative, in-demand |

## The Promise

The brand promise is what you will use to set yourself apart from the competition. Too many companies make the mistake of dismissing their brand's promise. That's a terrible idea because consumers take it very seriously. Empty slogans are a successful brand's worst enemy. You must deliver on your word, or your audience will walk away and never look back.

This is a tough challenge for a team. Do you promise a winning season or a good time? Your promise must not only be calculated, it must fit your archetype, Walkaways and message points, too. And you will want it to be something that can be sustained for an entire season (or, for sponsors, an entire campaign) no matter what happens. (For more on message development, see Chapter 6.)

Another important thing to consider when designing your brand promise is how to announce that pledge to your consumers. If it isn't obvious to them, it might as well be non-existent. Make sure that as soon as someone sees your marketing materials, or encounters you at a game or event, that they know right away what differentiates you from everyone else and why they need you.

While there is no magic formula for successful re-branding, if you strike the right balance between the five elements of a thriving brand, you will set yourself apart in the minds of the fans. Characters, archetypes, Walkaways, personality and promise all combine to create a strategy that speaks directly to consumers—and keeps them at your side for the long haul.

*"How you respond to the challenge in the second half will determine what you will become after the game, whether you are a winner or a loser."*

Lou Holtz

# Brand Audits

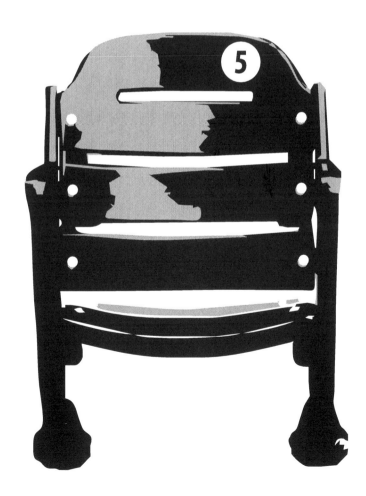

**A brand audit is the process of assessing how your brand is perceived by the public - its strengths and weaknesses.**

There are those organizations that already have all (or most) of the elements of a successful brand. It's possible that you are holding the pieces you need to get noticed— all you need to do is find a better way to make those pieces fit.

A brand audit is the process of assessing how your brand is perceived by the public—its strengths and weaknesses—and what you can do to "tweak" that perception in your favor.

Using the branding basics from Chapter 4, you can apply those concepts to your own brand audit in order to decide if you need to start over with your branding, or if a little careful editing will do the trick.

### Brand Element #1: Character

Start by reviewing your materials and the message you're sending. Who are the characters in your current message? (Or is there a lack of cohesive storytelling altogether?) It's important not to try and be everything to everyone. Instead, keep in mind the fairytales of youth. The following elements of good stories work just as well for a brand or sponsorship as they did for Snow White.

- There is always a clearly defined hero and antagonist.

- The storyline pivots around the hero (often the underdog) defeating someone (or something) big and bad.

- Additionally, there are usually some supporting characters,

beneficiaries and a benefactor or
two thrown in.

- The story is clearly defined.

*Example of character as a brand element:*

In 1984 (much to the horror of his company's directors), music entrepreneur Richard Branson launched Virgin Airways. Determined to develop a unique and more enjoyable way to fly, Branson simultaneously created some of the most well-developed characters in modern marketing history, casting himself in the role of benefactor. His "hero" may not have ridden in on a white horse, but Virgin certainly had its work cut out anyway. Big, impersonal airlines—and their stodgy image—made the perfect foil to the always irreverent chairman. Telling his brand's story in a way that resonated with travelers crying out for alternatives in air travel, he padded the tale with a cast of supporting characters that included flight attendants who actually made it fun to spend time in the air. Following through with his promises to shake up the way people fly, Branson even managed to turn his planes (and flights) into characters for this ever evolving story. From a hilarious take on the in-flight safety video that's shown before every take off, to the modern, comfortable décor of every plane, Branson has created a completely new take on flying—one that consumers don't mind paying a premium for.

## Brand Element #2: The Walkaways

Because Walkaways are the statements and sentiments (verbalized or not) that consumers carry with them after any transaction with your organization, a great way to "check up" on them is to put yourself in the mindset of a potential fan or customer. In order to understand how your brand is communicating with the audience, write down about six messages that are consistently transmitted by your brand. Be sure your Walkaways are always written from the perspective of the consumer.

If you can't come up with any, then your audience is probably not taking anything away from interactions with your brand either. If you come up with more than six, your Walkaways might be getting lost in information overload. Trimming down the amount of messages that you send will help the essential ones stand out.

*Example of Walkaways as a brand element:*

International Business Machines knew what they wanted their Walkaways to be. They wanted every customer, client and potential consumer to associate two words with every transaction they had with the company—speed and dynamics. In 1972, after a successful brand audit, they streamlined every aspect of their messaging and PR. Keeping simplicity and originality in mind, they even shortened the name of the company and its logo. IBM remains one of the most well-known (and well-respected) brands in the world today.

Possible IBM Walkaways:

- IBM is one of the most trusted names in business in the world today (1972).

- I associate the name IBM with speed.

- IBM is about dynamics.

- IBM is my choice for any machine necessary to do business.

### Brand Element #3: Archetypes

What archetypes are being conveyed in your messaging? Using the descriptions from Chapter 3, try to identify one or two archetypes that emerge from your current marketing efforts. (Don't be alarmed if you don't see a clear answer; most organizations are not yet taking advantage of the inherent simplicity of archetypes.) Once you know your archetype, it should be easy to determine your characters and Walkaways.

*Example of archetypes as a brand element:*

Recognizing the power behind archetypes, Starbucks Coffee is a living, breathing example of its explorer image.

**Consumers will put a lot of stock in the promises and slogans that you present to them, and they will hold you to every one of them.**

Named after the first mate on the whaling ship in Melville's classic Moby Dick, Starbucks brings its seeking explorer archetype to every aspect of the company. The logo (a sea siren) brings to mind images of sea-bound adventures and crashing tides, while the products themselves are as individualized as the "adventurers" that drink them. Each drink becomes whatever you want—bringing endless possibilities to the explorers that order them. The key here is to consistently make the idea of the archetype flow through every aspect of the company, from marketing and branding to the customer's name on each cup of coffee. Everything should signify that an individualized product was created exactly the way the consumer dreamed it up.

## Brand Element #4: Personality

In your current campaign collateral and branding, what type of personality is being conveyed? Try this exercise: Write down the top five or six traits that you see (or would like to see) consistently executed in your materials. Don't forget to use traits that would describe a person. In other words, avoid terms like "time tested" or "tried and true," because you wouldn't describe a friend using those words. The idea here is to see how human your brand is right now and to make adjustments accordingly.

*Example of personality as a branding element:*

Nearly 100 years ago, the Hall Brothers created a simple line of greeting cards that carried the family name on the back. In 1944, as the company struggled to stay afloat, marketing executive C.E Goodman locked himself in his office and tried to capture the essence of what put Hallmark greeting cards above the rest. On the back of a 3X5 card, he jotted down the phrase, "When you care enough to send the very best." Little did he know that his scribbling would become one of the best known and loved slogans in the marketing world. Even as it put pressure on the company's employees to create "the very best," it created a sense of kinship between the product and the consumer. Today, Hallmark cards are the bestselling greeting cards in the world and the Hallmark television channel is synonymous with family friendly programming. The entire brand, in fact, has a sincere and genuine personality that is down-to-earth, warm and old fashioned. The fans of Hallmark consider the brand to be part of their own family.

## Brand Element #5: The Promise

You have to walk the talk—it's just that simple. If your promises don't hold up, your brand will quickly begin to lose its luster. And once you've lost your audience's trust, getting it back can prove to be trickier than you might realize. Consumers will put a lot of stock in the promises and slogans that you present to them, and they will hold you to every one of them. Choose your assurances carefully and be prepared to stand by each one. Never make promises that you know you won't be able to keep. And whatever you do, don't underestimate your audience.

*Example of the promise as a branding element:*

> After British Petroleum merged with Amoco, the oil giant presented the public with its new corporate identity as a socially conscious and forward thinking company. Acknowledging the threat of global warming, the company began to associate its name with the term "Beyond Petroleum," expressing a shift in thinking and the company's desire to find alternative and environmentally friendly energy sources. The marketing campaign was wildly successful—until a series of oil spills gave the public reason to question the company's real dedication to being eco-conscious. Public opinion of BP soon soured as many people began to see BP's branding adjustments as a mask and not their true persona. Today, the company is struggling to regain a favorable public image.

## In Summary

It's not always necessary to uproot and start over. The basics for a wildly successful brand or sponsorship campaign may already be at your fingertips. Don't underestimate the importance of clever editing.

*"Adversity will cause some men to break; others to break records."*

William A. Ward

# Branding and Message Development

**A marketing campaign and its message need to be flexible enough to work for your organization regardless of what happens for them during the season.**

When it comes to the promises you make with your brand, the way you get your message across is just as important as what you're trying to say. Promising a winning season or a stellar performance may seem like a great idea until your team starts playing like the team in the film "The Bad News Bears," or until a player makes a wayward ethical decision.

Take for example the story of the Philadelphia 76ers in the 1970s. Beating longtime rivals the Boston Celtics in a seven-game playoff, Philadelphia advanced to the Eastern Conference Finals, thrilling 76ers fans throughout the country. There, they defeated the Houston Rockets (led by Moses Malone, a future player for the 76ers) in six games to advance to the NBA finals. Then they lost to the Portland Trail Blazers in six games; even after building an impressive 2-0 series lead.

This would eventually lead to the now infamous 1977-78 motto "We owe you one," a branding message that backfired in the worst way when Philadelphia lost in the playoffs that season to the Washington Bullets (the Bullets won the NBA championship.)

While "We owe you one" would have worked beautifully if the 76ers had gone on to win the playoffs, the truth was that no one knew what would happen throughout the year. A marketing campaign and its message need to be flexible enough to work for a team regardless of what happens for them during the season.

The real key to message development is blending your campaign with the season, basing the entire premise on the previous information from Chapter 4. Determine your archetype and then take the character, Walkaways and messaging, and blend it all into a campaign that resonates with your team's most loyal fans.

Keep in mind that your team's archetype should remain generally consistent from year to year. Otherwise, changes to the base personality will confuse followers and ultimately dilute the brand. If you're looking for variety from season to season, look within the archetype for the myriad of ways that an archetype can act while still remaining true to its base personality.

It's important to note that there is a difference between a brand and a marketing campaign. Your brand is who you are, the foundation upon which you will build your name and personality. Marketing campaigns are the extensions of the brand that you share with fans and consumers. While your marketing can (and should) change seasonally, your brand won't.

You can wear jeans and a tee shirt today and a three piece suit tomorrow, but your friends would still recognize you. Why? Because you're still the same person even if you dress differently. There's room to play as long as you don't change the essence of "who" your brand is.

Coca-Cola is one of the best representations of the innocent archetype in marketing history. From "teaching the world to sing" to adorable animated polar bears, Coca-Cola's advertising ventures have taken many different forms, all of them in keeping with the brand's feel and story. The only trial run that wasn't successful? New Coke. New Coke went against everything that the brand stood for: tradition, family and fun. It went against the very grain of its own brand.

Regardless of a team's performance throughout a season, the brand message should still ring true. And, if you're lucky, the messaging, the team, the brand and the sponsorship will blend together so seamlessly that the line that distinguishes one from the other will all but disappear.

Consider for a moment what many have called one of the greatest taglines in all of sports marketing history: "Just do it."[1]

Nike's groundbreaking advertising campaigns used that one line to catapult the brand to superstar status. Suddenly, it didn't matter if you were a man or a woman. It didn't matter if you were a basketball big

## Embrace your archetype and develop a slogan, motto or campaign that will resonate.

shot earning seven figures or a guy shooting hoops with his work buddies at the gym. It didn't matter if you were running for a gold medal or a woman trying to lose post-pregnancy baby fat. No matter your situation, the campaign defined you as an athlete and urged you to claim your moment in history. Don't think about it … just do it.

The "Just do it" campaign did exactly what it set out to do: It captivated the hero in all of us and made everyone feel like it was perfectly rational to spend a small fortune on a pair of athletic shoes in the name of heroism. The message captured the soul of the product so well that it became a brand in and of itself. Posters, billboards, parodies, magazine spreads and television spots are all testaments to the power that this simple brand message still holds over the public today.

That's exactly what you want for your brand, team or sponsorship: staying power and effectiveness.

Any successful marketing campaign will be made up of the same three basic elements as a successful organization: a properly selected market, an appealing message and excellent timing.

**Market:** Once you've concluded your brand audit, you should have a pretty good concept of your market and who your brand is. You've narrowed down who your characters aren't, and that is a crucial first step in the formation of your brand's story. You've also embraced your target audience. Now you have the opportunity to be playful with the information you gathered. How well do you know your audience? What do they like?

More importantly, what message can you offer that will make them feel an affinity with your brand?

**Message:** The message shouldn't be all about your players or team. Embrace your archetype and develop a slogan, motto or campaign that will resonate with those who are already faithful followers, or with those who will recruit new ones. Work your understanding of your audience's wants, hopes and fears into your brand's message. (This is the way that Nike got into the head of athletes everywhere and convinced them that the shoe giant was speaking directly to them, on a personal level.)

**Timing:** What's the difference between a slimy pile of old vegetables and a crisp garden salad? The same thing that differentiates a successful marketing campaign from a potential flop: timing.

Like all markets, your target audience will go through waves of change. In other words, there are certain times when your fans will be more receptive to certain ideas than others. For example, fans may have been much more receptive to community-building events in the months after 9/11 than any other time in history.

Recognizing these moments and acting on them can play a huge role in the take-off and success of your brand's message. (If you don't think you need a new couch today, you will most likely ignore television and magazine ads for furniture stores. But after your rambunctious nephew and his drooling bulldog spend the weekend at your house, you are probably going to be a lot more amenable to the idea of a new and less sticky place to watch TV.)

You want your campaign to be flexible enough to ride the waves of events that may occur during any season and be memorable enough to stick with people long after they've left the stadium or turned off the TV.

After all, the Dallas Cowboys are still known as "America's Team" long after the "personality" that brought on this nickname has dissipated. Doesn't your brand deserve the same longevity?

*"The other teams could make trouble for us if they win."*

Yogi Berra

# Telling Your Story Visually

**When deciding how to convey your message visually, it's important to take into account that every detail will have some kind of effect on the viewer.**

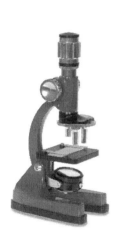

Like the vivid pages of a graphic novel, the visual design of your brand helps convey the story of your marketing campaign. In fact, graphic design can be one of the best ways to get your organization's message across to its customers. Your brand and its archetype can (and should) be translated into a visual version. Consider it the illustrated chapter in your brand's story. When deciding how best to convey your message visually, it's important to take into account the fact that every detail will have some kind of an effect on the viewer.

What follows are some ideas to consider as you lay out your visual design plan.

### Color Cues

More than just splotches of ink, the colors you choose for all of your visual elements are almost as important as the message itself. Some colors induce physical reactions in viewers, while others hold important cultural or social significance. Still others are forever linked to past trends in marketing and advertising. (Is anything more synonymous with kitchens of the 1970s than the color avocado green?)

For example, as the color of fire, red is a very emotionally intense hue. Used to symbolize everything from power and courage to energy and sexuality, red has been scientifically proven to increase a person's respiration rate, enhance metabolism and raise blood pressure. When used as an accent color, red stimulates the brain and brings pictures and text into the foreground.[1]

On the other end of the color spectrum, blue tones are linked to human consciousness and intellect. Dark blues, considered among the most masculine colors, are favored by corporate America, most likely because people subconsciously associate the color with precision, excellence, stability and intellect.[1]

Every color you use in your graphic design will likewise connect on various levels with your target audience.

Be aware of how you use colors and what colors are dominant in your marketing campaign or brand. Obviously it's important to stick to graphic standards and team colors, but it's important to be aware of what those team colors intrinsically say. Then, consider how adding new colors can emphasize your message and possibly give your brand some new life.

It's important to keep in mind that the meaning of colors varies depending on country, race and culture. This means it's essential to understand not only the colors you use, but the target market as well. For example, in the United States, the color white, a symbol of purity and new beginnings, is often associated with weddings. In Eastern cultures, white signifies death. You would go broke rather quickly if you decided to market white wedding dresses in China!

Here are some examples of what various colors communicate to your audience on the following page.

| | |
|---|---|
| **Red** | • Excitement, speed and strength   • Danger and anger<br>• Action, confidence and courage<br>• Passion, sensuality and love |
| **Brown** | • Nature, earthy connection and the stability this brings<br>• Relaxing, wholesome and confident<br>• Genuine and reliable |
| **Orange** | • Stimulation & increased creativity<br>• Relief from things becoming too serious<br>• Low cost and affordability   • Enthusiasm & cheerfulness |
| **Yellow** | • Sharper memory, attention-grabbing & concentration<br>• Summer, comfort, joy and liveliness<br>• Energy and clarity |
| **Blue** | • Calm, relaxation, solitude and peace<br>• Professionalism, loyalty, honor and trust<br>• Coldness and winter   • Open to communication |
| **Green** | • Reliability, durability and environmentalism<br>• Feeling a need for change and/or growth<br>• Spring-time, safety   • Harmony, freshness |
| **Purple** | • Extending imagination to its fullest<br>• Power and the ability to remove obstacles<br>• Royalty, nobility, elegance and luxury |
| **White** | • A fresh, new beginning<br>• Peace, innocence and purification<br>• Cleanliness, purity and sterility |
| **Black** | • Unknown and mystery<br>• Elegance, power and secretive<br>• Depression, morbidity and nighttime (emptiness) |

## Font Facts

While it may not seem particularly important at first, the selection of the right font can make or break a brand or marketing campaign. When it comes to print ads, billboards, web graphics and direct mail, you have a very small window of opportunity to grab and hold the public's attention. Very seldom will someone give your page a second glance if it didn't excite them right off the bat. While an old-world font or a calligraphy style might seem interesting in theory, they are pretty hard to decipher. And no one wants to have to struggle to understand what an ad is saying. Keep in mind that a simple font might be the best choice. Let your messaging speak for itself.

| Serif typefaces | Times Roman, Garamond, New Baskerville and Bodoni |
|---|---|
| Serif typefaces<br>Serif typefaces<br>Serif typefaces | *Serif fonts tend to be the most used in printed materials such as magazines, newspapers and books.* |
| **Sans Serif typefaces** | Helvetica, Arial, Futura, Gill Sans and Frutiger |
| Sans Serif typefaces<br>Sans Serif typefaces<br>Sans Serif typefaces | *Sans Serif fonts tend to be used more for display typography, such as headings, headlines, signage and situations that need legibility and readability. There are exceptions, as in this book.* |
| **Script typefaces** | Coronet, Brush and Zapfino |
| *Script typefaces*<br>*Script typefaces* | *Script fonts do not lend themselves for use in body text because they tend to be hard to read. They are typically used in logos and invitations.* |
| **Ornamental typefaces** | *Also known as novelty fonts, these are used mainly for decorative purposes and, at times, may incorporate objects and character designs in the type.* |

## Graphic Goodies

The average American is exposed to between 300 and 3,000 advertising messages every day. With competition that intense, you need a campaign that's so visually captivating that it can cut through the clutter and reach your audience on a personal level.

The graphic elements within your visual campaign are going to be the mortar that binds your viewing audience to your message. Strong images or elements that draw viewers in and reach them on a subconscious level are a necessity if you want your campaign to stand out in an over-saturated market. So, the question remains: how does your brand's graphic design impact your fans?

What is graphic design? Ask many people, and they will probably associate the term with complicated computer programs and drafting software. But the truth is that graphic design is everywhere, from the cover of this book to the label wrapped around the soft drink bottle sitting on your desk to the massive billboards you read as you're stuck in morning traffic. The point of all of these visual design elements is the same: to inform, persuade and attract. Simply put, graphic design is the marriage of art and technology, used in such a way as to capture the attention of your target market.

So now, armed with all of this new information, you're ready to tackle the concept of visual storytelling. It's time for a complete overhaul of your logo and image, right? Wrong!

While logos are important in terms of getting people to remember your name and associate you with a specific symbol (a psychologically proven trick to making yourself stand out in people's minds), logos don't have to be elaborate. Consider some of the most recognizable logos in the world: Microsoft Windows, McDonald's and Starbucks. With the billions of dollars in revenue that these marketing behemoths create annually, they could have come up with a newer, bigger and better logo by now, right? Those four colored squares don't really seem like inspiring technology, a giant golden M isn't going to fill up my stomach, and most people don't even know what is in the middle of that famous circle imprinted on their coffee cup. Truth be told, logos don't have to be glittery to be successful. They just have to be remembered by the people that see them.

Think back to some well-known sports brands that suddenly changed their logo and appearance (Capitals, Patriots, Pistons, Broncos, Blue Jays, 76ers, Rockets, and Boston College, just to name a few). While the change may have caused an initial increase in merchandise sales or brought about some new and fresh media awareness, it was undoubtedly a temporary swell in popularity. In the end, the facelift succeeded only in diluting the power behind the name and the original brand. There is a reason why fans still request merchandise with the original "retro" brand for those teams.

While some modifications to your logo can be ideal, especially if your current look isn't in sync with your story or archetype (compare the Arizona Cardinal's modified logo to their past logo), the real goal behind developing your graphic design and visual impact is to make your current brand stronger and more in tune with the fan's needs. That's why the strongest brands in the sports world haven't changed their logos in many decades. Names like the Cowboys, the Lakers, the Bears, the Celtics, the Red Sox and the Yankees, just to name a few, are synonymous with staying power and fan loyalty. The same holds true in the corporate sponsorship world. The biggest players in the advertising field haven't changed their logo because they haven't had to. Instead of changing their logo over the years, companies like Ford, Coors, Nike, State Farm, Budweiser and Rolex have concentrated their efforts on building up their story, archetype connection and overall brand.

Shouldn't your organization strive to model its branding after these giants?

Like a great story, strong visual appeal will draw loyalty and passion from fans no matter what the logo or outcome on the field.

*"Sports is human life in microcosm."*

Howard Cosell

# How to Build Your Brand During Tough Times

**People don't completely stop spending money during a recession, but they do look for better deals and smarter ways to spend it.**

It's on the news. It's on the radio. It's in the newspaper. It's all over the Internet. The sky is falling. In the face of a downward financial spiral, it can be hard to decide where to best spend your money. After all, the natural tendency for most people is to pull back during an economic crisis of any kind. And marketing is often the first department to feel the sting of the budget-cut knife. Unfortunately, that's one of the biggest mistakes an organization can make. Making smart moves with your marketing money during financially tough times can be the key to building lifelong loyalty to your brand by those consumers that already turn to you. And more importantly, this can be your biggest opportunity to attract a whole new set of faithful fans.

In times of economic downturn, most of your competitors will drastically reduce the amount of time and money they spend on their own marketing and advertising campaigns, clearing the way for you to aggressively market yourself. People don't completely stop spending money during a recession, but they do look for better deals and smarter ways to spend money.

Consider the Great Depression of the 1920s. One of the most trying times in U.S. economic history, it was also a period when some companies stepped up to the plate even as their rivals cut back on all advertising spending. Instead of cowering and waiting for product demand to begin climbing again, these brands created the demand themselves, allowing consumers to see that there were alternative ways to spend the money and still make ends meet. Customers felt abandoned by the large brands that seemingly dropped out of the public eye, associating the disappearing act with a lack of staying power. Consumers then turned to those brands that were being marketed aggressively and carried that loyalty with them long after the end of the Depression. For those brands that had previously been unknown, including names like Kellogg's, Ivory Soap, Chevrolet and Proctor & Gamble, the United States' harshest economic period turned out to be a boon.

Of course, just because your brand should be doing more marketing right now, doesn't mean that it should be doing the same kind of marketing.

Now more than ever, the focus of your marketing efforts should begin by thoroughly researching of your potential customers. Understanding how your target audience is responding to current market trends should be step one of your proactive marketing strategy. Beyond that, keep in mind that times of financial hardship shift many people's mindset back toward tradition and family values. Cozy scenes and affordable ways to spend time with loved ones are always big sellers, but never more so than when money is tight. For brands with archetypes that already focus on home and hearth (like the caregiver or the innocent) this is already a major part of their marketing strategy. However, every brand and sponsorship can tap into alternative ideas to bring friends and families closer—and fill seats in the process. (Consider promotions and "group deals" that consumers can use to associate your name with affordable family entertainment.)

Of course, knowing who to market to is only half the battle. If you don't adjust pricing techniques and product portfolios, all your careful research will be for nothing. That doesn't necessarily mean that your only option is to begin slashing ticket prices, but it might be a good time to carve out a few strategic promotional offers. Traditionally, harsh economic conditions have always lent themselves to successful group deals, season ticket sales and temporary pricing choices.

*"Some people are born on third base and go through life thinking they hit a triple."*

Barry Switzer

# Reaching
# Generation-Y

# Authenticity is king among young consumers. They can smell fake advertising a mile away.

When it comes to marketing to the so-called "connecteds" born between 1979 and 1995, you have your work cut out for you. But as these 71 million "Millennials" prepare to step up and replace the Baby Boomers as the largest force in the workplace (all the while spending well over $200 billion annually), can you really afford not to make a serious effort to reach them?

So just who is Generation Y and what makes them so different? Simply put, this is simultaneously the most optimistic and skeptical generation to ever walk the face of the planet.

We're talking about a group of young consumers who have already lived through everything from 9/11 and televised war to the Internet explosion and the text messaging revolution. Their DVRs let them fast-forward through commercials, they don't click on Internet banners and they ignore most magazine ads. How do you advertise to a demographic that refuses to work at a job unless it brings them personal satisfaction, or that considers social networking to be a religion or that sees right through 99 percent of all "clever" marketing techniques?

Let's start with a quick look at what doesn't work. When marketing to Generation Y, resist the urge to tell them what's cool. They will decide on their own—within seconds—if something is worth their time and attention. Nothing will turn this demographic off faster than someone talking at them instead of to them. Remember, this is a group of people who are constantly bombarded with information ... and are very selective about which of those messages they take to heart.

Who are the lucky few to get the Millennial's attention? Those that understand the one thing that they respond to: an experience. They don't want a product and they don't want to hear a pitch. They want something that is going to make an impact on their life (preferably wrapped up in an affordable and fast package). And when they find something that fits the bill, they want it instantly.

Take a look at some of the companies that have successfully marketed to connecteds—Red Bull, Mountain Dew, DC Shoes, and the holiest of all Generation Y brands, Apple. The entire iPod concept is the perfect example of the right way to reach Millennials: Offer them instant music downloads for 99 cents or so. In other words, give them a fast, affordable experience. Bingo.

So how do you recreate this success with your own brand or sponsorship? Begin by making sure that your entire marketing strategy can be summed up by one word: real. Authenticity is king among young consumers. They can smell fake advertising a mile away. When it comes to your brand, keeping it real may mean being cool, dorky, goofy, funny or sexy, but whatever it is, don't fake it.

You simply cannot market to Generation Y people until you understand their perspective on life. Take a quick breeze through MySpace or Facebook, and you'll begin to see a taste of this perspective. Community is important to them, and they take endorsements from friends as gospel. They take advice with a heaping tablespoon of salt and would rather text than talk.

Forget what you've heard about MTV, VH1 or BET. (Oh, and if you're considering a mass email campaign, you might want to think again. Unless you're a friend or co-worker, that email will most likely end up in the trash bin before it's even been opened). Instead, take your marketing off TV and put it into their hands. Here are a few examples of how to do that.

## Outdoor/Nature-Driven Events

As the generation in charge of reversing years of poor ecological care, Millennials will often jump at the chance to take part in outdoor or eco-friendly events.

## Concerts

Music is in Generation Y's DNA. Pop, rock, R&B, country or hip hop … if it's got a good beat, they will come.

## Extreme Sporting Events

The unprecedented success of events like the X Games and the Dew Tour prove that extreme (and non-traditional) sporting events hold a huge appeal to young consumers. Skateboarding/BMX competitions will almost always draw a big crowd.

## Social Networking Sites

Using Facebook, MySpace, Twitter, DIGG and del.icio.us is a surefire way to attract the attention of Generation Y. Just be sure that you keep it real.

Earn their respect and Millennials will prove to be your most loyal consumer base.

*"We are inclined that if we watch a football game or baseball game, we have taken part in it."*

John F. Kennedy

# Why Invest in a Sponsorship?

**The simple fact is, when it comes to brand exposure and return on investment, it's hard to beat the benefits of a well-executed sports sponsorship.**

The idea of a sports sponsorship isn't a new one. In ancient Greece, prominent merchants would create a show of support for athletes and, in turn, spectators would frequent their shops more often.

But is a sponsorship the right move for your organization?

The simple fact is, when it comes to brand exposure and return on investment, it's hard to beat the benefits of a well-executed sports sponsorship. But unless you go into the experience well-informed, you might lose out on some of the payback that drew you to sponsorship in the first place. No matter how alluring the thought of working with a team, athlete or event might be, it's only going to help your brand if it fits within your marketing plan and resonates with your ideal demographic.

### Why sponsor?

Is it worth it? Do the benefits outweigh the costs? Is a sponsorship different than an advertising campaign? The answers to these (and all other sponsorship questions you might have) could come as a pleasant surprise.

Before I get into some of the reasons why you can't afford not to consider sponsoring an event or team that appeals to your target audience, let's take a moment to dispel a couple of sponsorship myths. Here's a look at what a sponsorship isn't.

*A sponsorship is not advertising.*

Yes, a sponsorship will probably include some form of media exposure (like television/news broadcasts or magazine spreads), but it's very different from advertising. Advertising, a quantitative medium, involves payment to have a product or idea presented to the public. It directly promotes a company with the purchase of air-time or ad space exclusively for that purpose. Sponsorship, on the other hand, involves payments that contribute to some or all of the cost of an event (usually requesting that their product or organization receive prominent display space in return). It's this very difference that causes many people to consider an integrated sponsorship more credible in the eyes of the consumer than an outright advertisement.

*A sponsorship is not philanthropy*

Even if a sponsorship's recipient is a non-profit organization, it's important not to confuse it with an act of philanthropy. Charity is the support of a cause without a single commercial incentive. Those considering a sponsorship are most likely doing so with the purpose of achieving one or more commercial objectives.

So, while some of the benefits typically offered by both philanthropy and advertising are mirrored within the qualitative medium that is sponsorship, there are still some advantages to sponsorship. These advantages include interaction with potential clients, access to a live audience and on-site promotions.

Here's why sponsorship might be the right choice for your organization.

## Connection with Consumers

Is there anything as important to your brand as enhancing your customers' (or potential customers') attitude towards your name?

Most people are accustomed to tuning out the hundreds of marketing messages that bombard them on a daily basis. But put those same people in an experiential environment and you've just lowered their guard enough to be able to catch their attention. Suddenly, they're associating your name with the great time they're having, even if it's on a subliminal level.

It's important to note that because consumers will associate your brand with what you're sponsoring, the event/team you choose to endorse must fall in line with your image and archetype. Your sponsorship will allow you to reach a specifically targeted niche market, and doing your homework will help ensure that it's the right niche.

### Heighten Your Visibility

Positive publicity and the right kind of exposure can get all of the right people talking about your organization. Not only will your sponsorship advertising be seen by the crowds at the event, media coverage can multiply this visibility. This can happen in ways that might otherwise be unaffordable or unavailable. If at all possible, maximize on this marketing tool by promoting your team or event through your own public relations channels.

Additionally, a sponsorship's value is hugely augmented when you begin to activate it— heightening visibility through your own channels. For more on sponsorship activation, see Chapter 12: Sponsorship Activation.

### Set Yourself Apart

In the world of branding and marketing, a sponsorship can be a great equalizer that allows smaller or new companies to compete with industry giants and well-established brands. The mere act of sponsoring a team or event allows you to immediately differentiate yourself from the competition. This is a great way for you to make your name stand out, especially if your competition is working with a larger advertising budget than yours.

### Be the Good Neighbor

Society-minded brands often boost sales, especially among consumers who have

**It's important not to dilute your brand by agreeing to sponsor every event that comes along.**

strong ties to their communities, by contributing to local economic and social development. This will paint your organization in a positive light and appeal to your entire audience.

Corporate sponsorships are among the fastest growing marketing techniques in the United States.[1] Across the country, small and medium businesses are realizing what their larger counterparts have known all along: sponsorships drive sales. As a promotional tool, a sponsorship allows you to showcase your brand, without coming across as pushy. In fact sponsorships are one of the few advertising styles that allow you to come across as the good guy.

Additionally, sponsoring an event allows you to relate directly with your consumers. Suddenly, your product has become an integral part of an experience that they believe in. This creates the most valuable asset your organization could hope for: customer loyalty. Nothing can compete with an emotional association. Without the emotional attachment, every similar product and company is interchangeable. This sentimental factor is the one thing that can ensure that your organization stands out.

Are you still unsure about sponsoring?

Keep in mind that aside from considerably increasing your visibility, image and prestige, a sponsorship also offers unique solutions for connecting with other businesses, special consumers and potential vendors. These hospitality opportunities (including VIP receptions and special promotions) offer you exclusive networking possibilities, as well as the chance to solidify important business relationships.

## Be Selective

Keep in mind that while a sponsorship can be the best thing that ever happened to your organization, it's important to be careful not to dilute your brand by agreeing to sponsor every event that comes along. Sponsorship works best within the context of an ongoing relationship between your name and the event, person or team you sponsor. This is why you see so many big name brands sponsoring the same events year after year. You can afford to be selective in this area of your marketing strategy. Go with only the events that have an archetype, a philosophy and an image that mirrors your own brand's beliefs.

## Be Mindful

Of course, there are times when a sponsorship isn't the right move for your organization. For example, to make the most of your sponsorship you should expect to spend up to three times the amount of your initial sponsorship amount on activation. If that's not feasible, or if you find yourself stretching your company's budget to include the sponsorship in the first place, then the timing probably isn't right.

Here are some other reasons why a sponsorship might not be the best decision for you.

- A sponsorship needs the help of the sponsored organization, team or event to be successful. If your desired event doesn't have designated staff to serve your account, or if they can't help with your activation needs, then walk away.

- No one at a vegetarian festival is interested in hamburger meat, no matter how lean and delicious it is! A sponsorship needs to match not only your product, but your company's core beliefs as well. Take careful note of your target audience and only consider those events that cater to them.

- Does the sponsorship give you exclusivity in your category? If not, don't do it or at least expect less ROI.

- The most effective sponsorships will have a multi-year contract with additional options for future years along with agreed upon costs and right of first refusal for following years. Don't sign on unless you're sure of this.

Once the sole domain of only the largest and most influential companies, today's sponsorships are available to just about any brand—allowing them to reach a large circle of potential clients and decision makers in ways that they otherwise couldn't afford. If it looks like sponsorship is the right choice for your organization, then read on to find out about the importance of activation.

*"Sweat plus sacrifice equals success."*

Charlie Finley

# When Sponsorship is a Win-Win

**The most effective sponsorships build brand equity— linking the brand to archetypes that create an emotional response within your target audience.**

Say "sports marketing" and two images typically come to mind: athletes wearing corporate logos on their clothing or equipment, and stadiums ringed in signage touting various brands or services. While these kinds of endorsements will always play a part in sports sponsorship, today's sponsorship propositions demand something more than a logo displayed by an athlete or a logo prominently placed in a sporting venue.

The most effective sports sponsorships build brand equity—linking the brand to specific archetypes that create an emotional response within your target audience and create an effective "story" for your organization, thus providing a win-win association between the sponsor and sponsoree.

The challenge facing marketers today is how to enhance a sponsor's brand by ensuring that its customers have the right kinds of experiences with its products and services in the context of sponsorship.

Brand recognition and recall are keys, of course, but so are the less tangible links that connect a customer's experience with the archetypes and values which characterize a brand and differentiate it from its competitors. These links can be symbolic, experiential or functional, but they are essential to establishing a strong connection between the brand and its sponsored organization or event.

### Maximize Your Investment

With almost $9 billion spent on sports sponsorships in 2006 alone, sports is the largest category of sponsorship spending in North America. This number represents almost two-thirds of all sponsorship spending in the same year.

Experts predict that sports sponsorship spending will increase to over $13 billion by 2011, and continue to represent between 65 and 70 percent of overall sponsorship spending in North America.

At these spending levels, marketers must maximize their investment, leveraging dollars spent across a spectrum of consumer, trade, employee and media activities through sponsorship activation. As one expert has noted, "A company will only realize the full value of the sponsored property when it is used as a central platform around which [other] activities are built. Knowing how to leverage sponsorship is as much in the interest of the sponsored as the sponsors."

Organizations should not be afraid of the cost of sponsorship, but they should seek to make the most of their investment on every possible front. The Methodist Hospital of Houston's sponsorship of the Houston Astros MLB team is a prime example of this.

Methodist Hospital advertises heavily at Minute Maid Park, the Astros home field, but it also echoes the "team" and "competitor" symbolism in its institutional advertising and web presence. "There's one team in town passionate about being the best—this is the spirit at Methodist," say the ads for the Methodist Bone and Joint Center (home to the hospital's sports medicine clinics).

The center's web site boasts that its physicians are the official team doctors for the Astros and that they are dedicated to "Keeping Houston's best athletes—and you—playing strong and pain free."

Additionally, the Houston Astros are frequent visitors to various Methodist Hospital events and clinics. The hospital also picks up the tab for "Berkman's Bunch," a clubhouse gathering for at-risk children hosted by Astros' first baseman Lance Berkman before every home game at Minute Maid Park. Berkman is also the voice on Methodist Hospital's radio spots targeting services from cardiac care to wellness programs.

Methodist Hospital, which has the tagline "Leading Medicine," uses its association with the Astros to project that leading image through sports affiliation. It's the perfect example of a win-win sponsorship relationship. The team's archetype fits beautifully with its sponsor's—and the use of cause marketing and brand development by each side has only served to strengthen the sponsorship in the eyes of consumers.

Reliant Energy, name sponsor of Houston's Reliant Park and Arena, is also a sponsor of the NFL franchise Houston Texans. This is another great example of sponsorship done right.

**When a large percentage of a fan base is heavily involved in a product category, sponsorship is more likely to have a maximum impact.**

As venue sponsor, Reliant Park hosts more than 200 events each year. In keeping with its caregiver archetype, Reliant Energy has launched an initiative that will help make the Park more energy efficient, lowering the county's electric bill. This green marketing strategy is appealing to the area's largest population—young Americans. Green marketing and Generation Y go hand-in-hand.

In addition, the Greening of Reliant Park campaign is part of a much larger cause to help the City of Houston become more energy efficient, save resources and save money at the same time.

As a sponsor of the Texans, Reliant launched the Reliant Energy Power Players, which supports after-school flag football and homework programs for the Greater Houston Boys and Girls Clubs.

Also, eight Houston-area high school student athletes annually receive $1,000 scholarships as part of the Reliant Energy Scholarship for Champions—Powering Strong Minds and Bodies program. The winners of these

scholarships are selected by Reliant Energy and the Houston Texans, based on both academic and athletic performance, as well as strong leadership and commitment to ethics. This is cause marketing combined with sponsorship activation, a winning combination.

## Don't Forget the Fit

One crucial reminder for would-be sports sponsors: Don't get starry-eyed and zero-in on your favorite sport, team or athlete with little or no thought to your brand's target market.

How similar are your customers to the fan base of the sport, team or event you are considering? What competing companies in your market are doing sports sponsorships and with whom? Most importantly, are you willing to spend up to $3 in activation for every dollar spent on a sponsorship—up to 2 percent of your total marketing budget?

If the fit is there, the opportunities are great for success in both short-term sales building and longer term brand building. Experts suggest that the greatest success with sponsorships is realized when the following elements are in place.

- **Engaged fans are highly involved in the product/service category.** When a large percentage of a fan base is heavily involved in a product category, sponsorship is more likely to have a maximum impact. A NASCAR event is a better fit for the maker of shock absorbers or sports drinks than it is for a provider of home healthcare services!

- **The event is supported by serious money.** If a company hasn't invested at least as much in promoting the sponsorship as it has in acquiring the rights to an opportunity, the odds of success are not high.

- **The company uses the sponsorship to communicate a clear message about the brand to a responsive target.** Linking a brand to a team, sport or event to build brand awareness "in name only" is a poor investment. The connection between sponsorship and brand should embrace a common ideal or value, thus making the message as important as the property itself.

- **There is a clear link between the product and sponsorship.** When the connection is weak or stretched, impact is diminished. If it takes longer than five seconds to explain the connection between your brand and a sports marketing opportunity, most target buyers won't "buy it."

Sports sponsorships are not low-cost propositions. But they can be extremely rewarding, especially if the sponsoring organization has done its homework. Seasoned marketers know that the cost of reaching new customers can be 6-to-8 times the cost of maintaining and servicing existing ones.

The possibility for a win-win collaboration is high if the following factors are present: your organization's brand, story and archetype align readily with the target audience for a sports venue, team or event; you're willing to commit the funds and creative capital necessary to maximize the partnership; and the sports/event organization has an infrastructure that can support it.

*"If winning isn't everything,
why do they keep score?"*

Vince Lombardi

# Sponsorship Activation

**What better place to start creating a buzz about your new sponsorship than within your own company or organization?**

So, after careful research, some conscious budgeting and much planning, you've (finally!) finalized that sponsorship deal. Now what?

Simply putting a sponsorship program into effect isn't enough to reach your organization's objectives, much less drive sales in your direction. Enter sponsorship activation.

IEG Sponsorship Consulting defines activation (also known as leverage) as "the marketing activities a company conducts to promote its sponsorship. Money spent on activation is over and above the rights fee paid to the sponsored property."[1]

In other words, until you allocate some serious resources—time, staff and money—to letting both the fans and your targeted consumers know about the sponsorship, the sponsorship simply doesn't stand a chance of being successful. This is not something to consider only after you've embarked on your sponsorship deal.

As mentioned in the previous chapter, you should expect to spend up to three times the amount of your initial sponsorship investment on activation. But just what should you do with that money?

Simply put, you should be using your own channels to heighten the visibility of your newly developed sponsorship. And there is no shortage of opportunities for you to raise the public awareness of your organization's sponsorship endeavors.

Here's a look at some activation ideas and tools (you can tailor them to meet your own needs).

## Start from Within

What better place to start creating a buzz about your new sponsorship than within your own company or organization? Give your employees the first crack at working at or attending the event, or set up fundraisers or special promotions that revolve around your event. (Getting your staff involved at the event is a great way for your consumers to touch your brand or organization. What better evangelists than your own employees?)

## Email Blasts

A popular marketing technique, email blasts consist of an electronic mailing sent to everyone on your mailing lists at the same time.

Email blasts can be a great way to stay in touch with your customer base, letting them know about your new association with a team or event.

This is also a great way to pass along any deals, promotions or specials that your company might be offering in association with its new sponsorship. In fact, you can even share your mailing list with your sponsored property—pooling names in order to send out cross promotional material. (See cross promotion, below.)

Note: If you are planning an email blast marketing campaign, it's important to be up to date on current spam laws. Make sure that your emails are wanted and informative, and that customers have a way to opt out of them.

Also, as mentioned in Chapter 9, email blasts do not work when marketing or branding your organization to the Generation Y crowd.

## Cross Promotion

When done well, cross promotion between your company and the team you are sponsoring can benefit both organizations, all the while helping to stretch your activation and marketing budgets.

Cross promotion involves pooling the resources of the team and sponsor so that everyone wins. Be creative about the things that are already a part of your daily business and consider how they could be made more valuable when combined with the assets of the team.

Similarly, there are ways that your company and your sponsored property can use cross promotion to reach your mutual target customers more effectively, without causing a major dent in your budget.

Here are some ideas:

- Print joint promotional messages on all of your receipts and/or ticket sales.

- Hang posters and banners announcing your sponsorship, and place similar advertising around your sponsored events.

- Offer a reduced price, special promotion, enhanced service or convenience to those customers who also attend your sponsored events.

- Give a joint interview to local media.

- Give away tickets or products (or host a raffle-style event) at both your own business and on the day of the event.

## Signage

Considered a basic element of sponsorship and in-venue activation, signage is one of the most consistent ways to reinforce your brand. Not only are consumers exposed to your corporate signage while attending a game or event, but many times exposure is also gained on local and national television

**Promotional items or give-aways that don't convey anything related to your brand, are basically useless as a marketing tool.**

stations. Some of the basic signage options available for sponsors include:

- Naming rights
- Column wraps
- Parking lot banners
- LED boards
- Concourse floor graphics
- Stair graphics
- Gate signage
- Field tunnel covers
- Field walls
- Concourse banners or murals
- Super-screen advertising
- Scoreboard signage
- Outfield wall signage
- Rotational signage
- Concession signage
- Dasher Boards

## Give-aways & Promotions

Promotional "give-aways" are often the first thing that people think of when they begin setting up an activation plan. However, unless they are carefully executed (and specifically geared towards your target audience) this type of marketing can be ineffective.

It's not enough to simply give fans a present as an incentive for showing up to games—or even as a reward for loyalty. If those gifts have nothing to do with your brand, how can you expect them to drive revenue in your direction?

Promotional items or give-aways that don't convey anything related to your brand, or that don't have any connection to your organization, are basically useless as a marketing or advertising tool.

It is just as important to ensure that your giveaway is related to your organization as it is to make sure that your promotion is reaching the right people. Freebies that proudly display the name of your laundry detergent, no matter how fabulous it is, won't do much good during a sporting event with a predominantly male audience. That's not to say that there is no such thing as a successful product give-away campaign.

**The more your audience correlates the fun they're having at an event with your organization the greater the benefit to your brand.**

Many of the top car racing teams use a variety of these techniques to establish a relationship with fans.

Beginning with a show car—a replica of an actual race car—they tour shopping centers and other locations where their target audience can be found. There, the fans can not only check out the car, but they can also pick up autographed memorabilia and occasionally meet the drivers.

Some teams even develop specialty products tied into the racing circuit. For example, Kellogg's Corn Flakes boxes have featured the company's sponsored NASCAR drivers, and these boxes have become collectibles.

### Viral Marketing

Viral marketing (and viral advertising) refers to the use of existing social networks to increase brand awareness and product sales. It's the epitome of word-of-mouth advertising.

Email is often considered the "father" of viral advertising. (It is, after all, still the best way for users to quickly forward messages and images to everyone they know.) But it's the success of sites like YouTube, Facebook, Digg, and Twitter that have proven viral marketing to be a global phenomenon.

*Example of viral marketing:*

> In December 2009, the Pentagon's Defense Advanced Research Projects Agency (DARPA) launched an online challenge. They offered a $40,000 prize to the first team that could locate 10 weather balloons hidden across the

country. The treasure hunt was set to last anywhere from several weeks to a few months.

Using social networking sites, a group of intrepid MIT students launched a viral campaign to assist in the location of the balloons. They offered incentives to those who were not only willing to provide information about balloon sightings, but also to those who could help get more people involved in the search.

It took these internet seekers less than nine hours to track down all 10 balloons and claim the prize.

It was a big win for the Massachusetts Institute of Technology—and a prime example of what good viral campaigning can accomplish.

A successful viral marketing campaign will often include many of the following strategies:

1. Giving away free products or services and giving the participants the ability to share or download.
2. Using common communication tools (think Twitter, YouTube, blogs, email, etc.).
3. Scaling the entire campaign to be based on your market and viral goals.
4. Making people feel something (emotional ties are crucial to getting consumer buy-ins).
5. Making it unexpected (consumers are more likely to remember something if it's funny or catches them by surprise).

Keep in mind that while it's not necessary to incorporate all of these elements, the more of them that you include, the higher the likelihood of a successful campaign.

## Billboards

I know what you're thinking: This seems like old-school marketing. After all, billboards have been around since the dawn of advertising. No one pays attention to them anymore, right? Wrong.

While it's true that a boring or traditional billboard is a complete waste of your marketing budget, an inventive and creative one can create buzz about your organization and sponsorship.

The Sacramento Kings, for example, launched a billboard campaign in October of 2009 to promote the upcoming season. They recruited 15 local artists and had each one create a hand-painted billboard that the Kings put up at various locations around the city. People are still talking about it (and it even made the local newscast).[2]

That kind of out-of-the-box thinking is the key to a billboard marketing campaign, one that will stand out in the consumer's mind. Here are few other ideas to contemplate.

### The Living Billboard

Who can forget the two Brazilian brothers who spent the summer of 2009 living 33 feet up in the air on the side of a building to promote a display at the art gallery where they lived and worked?

Not only did they create incredible word-of-mouth advertising, they became an internet sensation (viral marketing, anyone?).

Why not kick off a sale on season tickets by having your team mascot perform a similar stunt atop a billboard? Or, for a winter sports idea that's sure to catch attention, consider setting up a working ski lift between two adjacent billboards and have team players or mascots ride it several times a day.

### The Mystery Board

In 2004, internet giant Google took an unusual approach to the e-hiring concept. They posted several large billboards in the Silicon Valley, California area with complicated math equations on them. Nowhere in the advertisements did the search engine's name appear, but people who entered the correct answer into the Google home page were directed towards information on how to apply for a job with the famous web site.

Mysterious or funny billboards will stand out in the minds of fans and consumers, and that will lead to increased sales.

## Building Wraps

During repair and construction of London's St. Paul Cathedral, the entire façade was wrapped in an enormous poster that resembled the completed project. Tourists took pictures and enjoyed the "redone" church long before the construction crew was through.

Similarly, building wraps can be a great way to capture the attention of fans, consumers and passers-by. What larger canvas can you ask for than the side of a skyscraper?

Here are a few other ideas for your billboard or super-graphic:

- 3-D boards
- Animated or digital billboards
- Mobile boards
- Boards made with mixed materials
  (grass, dice, wood or your actual product)
- Interactive boards
- See-through boards
- Video boards
- Wrapping planes or vehicles
- Performance art boards

## Media Events & Public Relations

The more your audience correlates the fun they're having at an event with your company or organization (albeit subconsciously) the greater the benefit to your brand.

That's why it's essential to get your public relations department in on the sponsorship as quickly as possible. Positive PR is what is going to extend your sponsorship above and beyond the event itself. Consider creating special events around your team, coaches or even a particular athlete. (This works especially well when your consumers are actively involved in the event as well.)

For example, the 1994 winner of the Daytona 500, Sterling Marlin, competed in a lawnmower race against one of his biggest fans—a grandmother. Grandma may have emerged victorious from the race, but the real winner was the lawnmower company, which reaped the benefits of the publicity, including several television spots and news appearances.

## Hospitality

Hospitality events, also known as client entertainment, are an essential part of building a good relationship with key customers. While hospitality events in and of themselves don't guarantee repeat business, they do build client rapport, which is a necessity when it comes to making yourself memorable in a customer's mind.

These events include inviting key customers, clients, employees, government officials and other VIPs to an event. Usually this involves providing tickets, parking, dining and other amenities—often in a specially designated area. (Think pro-am sports, backstage tours, meet and greets, etc.)

As a sponsor, hospitality events give you the opportunity to have clients and customers, both current and potential, as a captive audience in a suite, a VIP box or at a pre-game meal.

The most important part of organizing a hospitality event is making sure that you set up a "base camp" where you can entertain and where your guests can get to know each other.

Client entertainment is the perfect platform for branded give-aways and event related promotional materials. (Again, make sure that your take-homes are valuable to your clients so they won't end up forgotten in the car trunk.)

Companies often use their sponsorships as venues to entertain valuable customers. Every major sporting event from golf to car racing has a VIP section set aside where these clients are treated to food, drink and a place to duck out of the sun or snow.

*"Even if you're on the right track, you'll get run over if you just sit there."*

Will Rogers

# Cause Marketing

## Find a cause that fits within your brand's story and, most importantly, that resonates with your target audience.

Cause marketing—the act of linking your brand or organization to a non-profit—is a great way to give back to the community while boosting your bottom line. Unlike philanthropy, which traditionally involves a specific (and often one-time) tax deductible donation, cause marketing is not donation based. Instead, it's an ongoing relationship between you and the charity of your choice.

Teaming up with a non-profit creates benefits for both organizations that otherwise might not be available to either.

For example, associating your brand's name with that of a charitable cause will not only improve your customer relations and the way the public reacts to your name, it also opens up new marketing and advertising opportunities for you. Responsible brands—those that willingly give back to the community—are in a completely different class, according to those who matter most (the customers).

Good "corporate citizens" are always received well by consumers, especially younger buyers.

When surveyed, consumers between the ages of 18 and 30 were very clear in their increased desire to do business with those companies and organizations that are committed to giving back. Here's an interesting statistic from the Cone Millennial Cause Study in 2006: Given the opportunity to choose between two comparable items, nearly 90 percent of Millennials would choose a brand associated with a charitable cause (unless there was a large price difference).

The popularity of this idea has been steadily growing since its first major debut in 1983, when American Express donated a penny from every charge made by cardholders towards restoring the Statue of Liberty. That innovative marketing strategy generated a couple million dollars for Lady Liberty's facelift and glowing press (and plenty of sales) for American Express.

Today, close to $1.6 billion is spent annually on cause-related marketing.

Sports brands and organizations are almost tailor-made to get the most out of a cause marketing campaign. Americans love their sports heroes. And when one of those heroes does something especially heroic, it only serves to reaffirm their passion. It's that kind of fervor that fuels the millions of dollars spent by sports fans every year.

*Example of cause marketing:*

> Norman Julius "Boomer" Esiason, former quarterback for the Cincinnati Bengals, the New York Jets, the Arizona Cardinals and current CBS sports commentator, is perhaps one of the biggest champions of cause marketing in the sports world.
>
> In 1993, while attending a training camp for the Jets, Esiason found out that his then two-year-old son, Gunnar, had been rushed to the hospital. The diagnosis was heartbreaking: cystic fibrosis.
>
> Soon after, the football hero formed the Boomer Esiason Foundation—a non-profit charity dedicated to researching a cure for cystic fibrosis, as well as educating people about the disease, and helping improve the quality of life of those who have been diagnosed.
>
> Fundraisers were great, but the business savvy Esiason and his wife soon realized that they could double their exposure and reach a much broader audience if they could piggy-back their efforts onto other, already established brands.
>
> Cause marketing has been the backbone of the BEF's success ever since.
>
> From Johnsonville Brats and Ebay to Jiffy Lube and Boomer Bar B Que sauce, literally dozens of companies have signed on to help spread the word about the organization.
>
> The result has been a definite win-win: Not only are these brands

enjoying marked increases in sales during the cause marketing campaigns, but the foundation has been able to raise more money (and increase more awareness) than it ever would have been able to do on its own.

As for Gunnar, he is now an active young adult, thanks in no small part, to the efforts of his doctors, parents and the foundation started in his name.

Like any major business undertaking, executing a successful cause marketing campaign can be tricky. As you forge a new relationship between your brand and a charitable organization, it's important to keep some rules in mind.

Remember, the goal is to create a "win-win" situation.

You want your customers to feel that by buying your product, they are doing something good, making a difference, helping those in need or otherwise improving the state of the world.

In return, you gain a reputation for caring and you become known as a responsible, socially conscious brand while enjoying increased exposure and sales.

Meanwhile, the non-profit generates awareness for their cause, and their own name gets a little extra exposure of its own.

See … everybody wins.

But it's essential that you align yourself with a charity with an archetype and image that is in synch with your own. Like a sponsorship, cause marketing campaigns must be involved with non-profits that share your organization's views, or it won't work. A leather goods store, for example, won't get very far by partnering with a charity that promotes a vegan lifestyle!

Instead, find a cause that fits within your brand's story and, most importantly, that resonates with your target audience. The best cause marketing campaigns are those in which the mission of the non-profit really echoes that of the sponsoring organization.

It's also important to remember that the average American consumer comes equipped with a finely tuned BS detector. Never insult the intelligence of your potential customers by supporting an issue that you don't really care about. They will catch on. A genuine passion and interest in a cause is essential for a successful partnership.

Once you find a charity that jives with your own organization's values, then you're ready to design your cause marketing campaign. Decide up-front what you want to get out of your new partnership, and then design a plan that will be mutually beneficial to you and your chosen non-profit.

Don't forget to factor in both tangible and non-tangible benefits. For example, you might decide that you want to see increased sales and publicity (including major visibility at games and charity events) as well as strengthening customer loyalty, building your brand name, enhancing your reputation and even improving your own employees' sense of pride in your company.

In fact, cause marketing is a good way to improve your employee retention rates. The Cone survey reported that over 70 percent of employees wished that the company they worked for did more in the way of charity work.

And keep in mind that although you are working with a charity, it is a marketing effort; so don't be shy about spreading the word. In addition to your current advertising technique, make sure you send out emails, host an event or two and let everyone know about your new venture. Now is not the time to be modest!

*"It's not whether you get knocked down; it's whether you get back up."*

Vince Lombardi

# Game On

## Only sponsor events whose archetypes, philosophy and image mirror your brand's.

Congratulations!

You're ready to take all that you've learned in the previous chapters and put it into practice. Keep in mind that while successful marketing doesn't require you to be a rocket scientist, it does call for a bit of trial and error. What's important is that you continue to tap into the ideas in this book and develop a successful campaign. Here's a quick review of some of the key pieces to the branding puzzle. There are four things to work through as you develop your strategy.

### Tell Your Story

This is where the importance of building your brand's story comes in. Stories live on long after the details have been forgotten. And nothing motivates and captivates people like a good story.

A quick, clever story will capture your audience's attention and hold it in a way that few other techniques can. Use a strong cast of characters and you'll have a strong beginning. The best place to find that cast is by tapping into the following 12 archetypes:

- The innocent
- The explorer
- The sage
- The outlaw
- The magician
- The hero
- The regular guy/gal
- The lover
- The creator
- The jester
- The caregiver
- The ruler

## What's Your Brand?

By definition, a brand is "The complete set of images about an organization held in the mind of the supporter." Who are those supporters? They are the sports fans, the home audience, the consumers who buy your product and the spectators whose attention you are trying to captivate.

As you attempt to find the invisible connective tissue that will bind your target audience to your name, remember that it is your brand that will catch their attention—and hold it.

## Who's Your Audience?

Now more than ever, the focus of your marketing efforts should begin by researching your potential customer base. The first step of a successful proactive marketing strategy is to understand how your target audience will respond to current market trends.

Beyond that, remember that times of economic struggle will shift the mindset of many people, causing them to crave tradition, family and nostalgic scenes of warmth and comfort.

But even well-told stories run the risk of becoming stale or outdated. If you feel that it might be time to re-brand, ask yourself some key questions.

- **What's my message?** Can consumers quickly see what you're trying to say? Is your message consistent, clear and concise?
- **Is my information current?** Outdated or unchecked facts are a branding disaster. Is your message fresh and informative?
- **Am I being consistent?** Are you keeping a common look, feel and vibe throughout all media and marketing collateral? Does it follow a consistent pattern?
- **Am I communicating well?** Is your target audience "getting" your message? Are you coming across in an engaging way? Are you interacting with your audience?

## Your Sponsorship

While a sponsorship can be the best thing that ever happened to your organization, it's essential that you not dilute your brand by agreeing to sponsor any event or team. A sponsorship works best when it's within the context of a healthy relationship between you and the sponsored team, event, organization or athlete. (That's why you see so many big names sponsoring the same event year after year.) You should be very selective about who or what you sponsor.

Only sponsor events whose archetypes, philosophy and image mirror your brand's.

Choosing the actual sponsorship is only half the battle. Activation, also known as leverage, are the marketing activities that you use to promote that sponsorship. And unless you're willing to allocate time, staff and cold, hard cash towards letting consumers know about your new relationship, your sponsorship doesn't stand much of a chance of being a success.

As we draw to a close, consider one final question: What do you have in common with Michael Jordan, Starbucks, Michael Phelps, Nike, Jeff Gordon and Apple Computers? Like them, you're just one person or organization on a quest for greatness. They did it and so can you.

Game on!

# NOTES

## Chapter 1

1. Times Online: The Anatomy of a Champion, July 1, 2009, http://www.timesonline.co.uk/tol/sport/olympics/article4526254.ece

2. 2008 Men's Basketball Attendance Charts (The NCAA News) July 5. 2009, http://www.ncaa.org/wps/ncaa?key=/ncaa/ncaa/ncaa+news/ncaa+news+online/2008/assocationwide/mens+basketball+adds+rung+to+attendance+ladder+-+05-16-08+ncaa+news

## Chapter 2

1. The Man Who Shot Liberty Valance directed by John Ford (California, Paramount Pictures 1962)

## Chapter 3

1. Princeton Wordnet Search, September 3, 2009, http://wordnetweb.princeton.edu/perl/webwn?s=archetype

2. Reference Answers, Answers.Com, September 3, 2009

3. Margaret Mark and Carol S Pearson, The Hero and the Outlaw (New York: McGraw Hill, 2001) p4

4. Oakland Raider Fans: Loony, Legendary, or Both? September 5, 2009 http://bleacherreport.com/articles/107363-oakland-raiders-fans-loony-legendary-or-both

## Chapter 4

1. The Business of Sports Management, August 15, 2009, http://www.booksites.net/download/chadwickbeech/Glossary.htm

2. Marty Neumeier, The Brand Gap (California: New Riders, 2006)

## Chapter 6

1.  Patrick Hanlon, Primal Branding (California: Free Press, 2006) p4

## Chapter 7

1.  Color Psychology, August 18, 2009.
    http://www.infoplease.com/spot/colors1.html

## Chapter 10

1.  Lesa Ukman, IEG's Guide to Sponsorship (Chicago: IEG 2007)

## Chapter 12

1.  Lesa Ukman, IEG's Guide to Sponsorship (Chicago: IEG 2007)

2.  Unique Kings' Billboards Painted By Local Artists, November 3, 2009
    http://www.nba.com/kings/news/kings_local_artist_2009.html

# INDEX

## About the Author

### Adam Nisenson

An award-winning marketer and branding expert with experience since 1992, Adam Nisenson has consulted for such organizations as the Houston Astros, Houston Texans, PGA Tour, ESPN, Dew Action Sports Tour, Seattle Seahawks, Reliant Energy, the Sommet Group, and many others.

His knowledge of the internal workings of sports teams, and of corporate branding and messaging, enable Adam to create marketing strategies that drive results for sponsors and teams alike. He is known as an on-the-spot "idea guy" who finds unique, new ways to elevate market awareness, drive revenue, and increase attendance.

Adam is the founder and past president of Active Imagination, a sports/sponsorship branding firm. He continues to consult on marketing and activation strategy for sponsors and teams through his firm The Captivate Group.

4500886

Made in the USA
Charleston, SC
01 February 2010